W9-BTG-380

Kadambari Sinha
Conversational Hindi

Kadambari Sinha

Conversational Hindi

BUSKE

Bibliografische Information der Deutschen Bibliothek

Die Deutsche Nationalbibliothek verzeichnet diese Publikation
in der Deutschen Nationalbibliografie; detaillierte bibliografische Daten
sind im Internet über <http://dnb.d-nb.de> abrufbar.
ISBN 978-3-87548-572-1

Umschlagabbildung: © mauritius images.

© Helmut Buske Verlag GmbH, Hamburg 2010. Alle Rechte, auch die des aus-
zugsweisen Nachdrucks, der fotomechanischen Wiedergabe und der Über-
setzung, vorbehalten. Dies betrifft auch die Vervielfältigung und Übertragung
einzelner Textabschnitte durch alle Verfahren wie Speicherung und Übertragung auf Papier, Filme, Bänder, Platten und andere Medien, soweit es nicht
§§ 53 und 54 URG ausdrücklich gestatten. Druck und Bindung: Druckhaus
„Thomas Müntzer", Bad Langensalza. Printed in Germany. *www.buske.de*

Contents

4 खाना-पीना Food and drink

5 ख़रीदारी Shopping

6 स्वास्थ्य-संबंधी Health matters

7 नाते-रिश्ते Family relations

Preface

This book is meant for adult learners with a basic grounding in Hindi who wish to extend their knowledge of the language and improve their communicative fluency. It first appeared in 2007 in a German edition, as the idea of writing a conversation course grew out of my experience of teaching Hindi as a foreign language in Germany. I noticed that despite months, or even years, of assiduously studying grammar structures and vocabulary, my students were at an utter loss when it came to taking part in everyday conversations.

Hindi learners elsewhere might also have made the disheartening discovery that classroom and course book instruction, which tends to focus on grammar, does not prepare them for actually using the language in real life. This is because grammatical competence is only one element of communicative ability. Sociolinguistic competence is just as essential: participating in a conversation can be daunting if the learner is unsure of the right language to use in different social and cultural contexts. Communicating spontaneously and effectively involves making quick decisions about which expressions are appropriate in a particular situation and which utterances, though grammatical, are not acceptable in normal use. To develop this awareness, learners need to be exposed to authentic language use in a variety of contexts.

Conversational Hindi attempts to address this need. It uses conversations between native Hindi-speakers to present learners with vocabulary and grammatical structures in use in a wide range of everyday social situations. Its 45 dialogues aim to give readers a glimpse into the daily lives of three middle-class families living in Delhi. The language they use is colloquial, idiomatic Hindi, typical of educated urban Hindi-speakers, which mixes words and phrases from Indo-Aryan and Perso-Arabic sources. The topics of conversation will, I hope, be of practical use to visitors to India and provide some insights into Indian culture and customs in an enjoyable way.

How to use this book

Conversational Hindi is divided thematically into 15 chapters, each of which consists of two to four dialogues in Hindi. Each dialogue in Hindi is followed by an English translation which has been kept as close and literal as possible. At the end of each chapter there is a Hindi-English glossary which lists the words of each dialogue in the order of their appearance in the text. An alphabetical Hindi-English glossary containing all the words listed in the 15 chapters is provided at the end of the book. Readers should note that the glossary defines each word only in the context(s) in which it appears, ignoring its other dictionary meanings.

Thirty-eight dialogues are recorded on the accompanying CD. These are marked in the left margin at the beginning of the dialogue with the following symbol indicating the CD track number: **10**

The book can be used both in the classroom and for self-study. The dialogues are accessible at different levels, the only prerequisite being a thorough knowledge of the Devanagari script. There is no fixed order in which they should be read or listened to, though it might be useful to begin with the first chapter, which introduces the five main protagonists. Grammatical explanations have been excluded with a view to encouraging learners to recognise that grammar, if embedded in a suitable context, can be intelligible without analysis.

Users are free to devise their own approach to the materials in the book, depending on their individual needs and proficiency levels. Some suggestions are given below:

Listening repeatedly to the recorded dialogues will help learners become familiar with the rhythm, stress and intonation of spoken Hindi, and benefit even elementary level learners who may not understand everything. Speaking along with the recordings is also useful.

Students with higher proficiency might enjoy acting out the dialogues in pairs or small groups, an activity which will help them memorise recurrent idiomatic expressions and phrasing that they can re-use in similar situations.

A challenging exercise for advanced learners could be to try and reconstruct the Hindi dialogues from the English translations, using the glossary as help. Teachers using this as a classroom activity can follow up with a discussion of the students' different versions of the same content and use it to focus on lexical phrases.

Acknowledgements

The characters in the texts were brought to life on the CD by Abha Monde, Anil Kumar Velagapudi, Manik Bali, Richa Mathur and Saugato Datta. I am very grateful to them for agreeing to lend their voices to the recordings, and for their generosity with their time. I would like to thank my dear friend, Sushama Jain, who supplied many of the photographs in this book, for her involvement and her valuable comments. To my husband, Jochen, whose companionship, support, and good humour I can always depend on, I owe thanks beyond words.

Most importantly, I thank my mother, Krishna Sinha, a constant source of strength and inspiration, not only for her unwavering faith in me and any project I undertake, but for her active collaboration on this book. Her advice on the texts and her translations of them were invaluable, as was her enthusiasm at every step of the way. I dedicate this book to her.

Hamburg, February 2010   *Kadambari Sinha*

1
लोगों से मिलना–जुलना
Meeting people

1.1   मेहमानों का स्वागत

   नए पड़ोसी

अजय	नमस्ते। आप ही श्रीमती पल्लवी जैन हैं?
पल्लवी	जी हाँ, कहिये? माफ़ कीजिए, मैंने आपको पहचाना नहीं।
अजय	हम आपके नये पड़ोसी हैं। हमने दूसरी मंज़िल पर आपके नीचे वाला फ़्लैट लिया है।
पल्लवी	आइए, अंदर आइए! बैठिए।
अजय	मेरा नाम अजय कुमार है और यह है मेरी पत्नी आन्या।
आन्या	नमस्ते। आपसे मिलकर बहुत ख़ुशी हुई।

पल्लवी	अरे वाह! आप तो बहुत अच्छी हिन्दी बोलती हैं! लेकिन आप भारत की तो नहीं हैं, न?
आन्या	जी नहीं, मैं जर्मन हूँ। मैंने हाइडलबर्ग विश्वविद्यालय में हिन्दी सीखी।
पल्लवी	बहुत बढ़िया! अच्छा, तो आप लोग क्या लेंगे, चाय या फिर कुछ ठंडा?
आन्या	धन्यवाद, लेकिन चाय पीने फिर कभी आयेंगे, पल्लवी जी। आज हम लोग ज़रा जल्दी में हैं।
अजय	आज तो सिर्फ़ आप को परिवार सहित अपने गृह प्रवेश में बुलाने आए हैं। कल शाम सात बजे पूजा है, उसके बाद खाना। आप लोग आएँगे न?
पल्लवी	जी हां, अवश्य आएँगे। अगर आपको किसी भी तरह की मदद की ज़रूरत हो तो बताइएगा।
आन्या	आपका बहुत शुक्रिया। ऊपर वाले की मदद तो हमेशा चाहिए होती है!
पल्लवी	हाहा, बिलकुल ठीक कहा!
अजय	अच्छा, तो हम चलते हैं। नमस्ते।
पल्लवी	नमस्ते। फिर आइएगा।

1.1   Welcoming guests

New neighbours

Ajay	Hello. Mrs. Pallavi Jain?
Pallavi	Yes? Excuse me, I didn't recognise you.
Ajay	We're your new neighbours. We've just moved into the flat below yours on the second floor.
Pallavi	Do come in! Have a seat.
Ajay	I'm Ajay Kumar and this is my wife, Anja
Anja	Hello. I'm very pleased to meet you.
Pallavi	Oh, how wonderful! You speak Hindi very well! But you aren't Indian, are you?
Anja	No, I'm German. I learnt Hindi at Heidelberg University.
Pallavi	Splendid! Now, what would you like, some tea or a cold drink?
Anja	Thank you, but we'll drop in another time for some tea. We are in a bit of a hurry today.
Ajay	We came today to just to invite you and your family to our house-warming. We're having a religious ceremony at seven in the evening tomorrow, followed by dinner. You will come, won't you?

Pallavi	Yes, we certainly will. Do let us know if you need help of any kind.
Anja	Thank you very much. One can always use help from the one above!
Pallavi	Haha, rightly said!
Ajay	Well, we ought to get moving. Bye!
Pallavi	Goodbye. Do come again!

1.2 दोस्तों से मुलाकात

बस स्टॉप पर

अलका	नमस्ते, पल्लवी! तुम कैसी हो?
पल्लवी	नमस्ते, अलका! मैं तो बिलकुल ठीक हूँ, लेकिन तुम बताओ कि तुम्हारा क्या हाल-चाल है? कई दिनों से दिखाई नहीं दीं।
अलका	हाँ, मैंने दफ़्तर से एक हफ़्ते की छुट्टी ली थी।
पल्लवी	क्यों, ख़ैरियत तो है न? राहुल और बच्चे भी ठीक हैं?
अलका	हाँ, हाँ, हम सब मज़े में हैं। मेरे चाचा की लड़की की शादी थी इसलिए हम चारों जयपुर गए थे।
पल्लवी	अच्छा, तो शादी में गए थे तुम लोग। मज़ा आया?
अलका	हाँ, ख़ूब मज़ा आया। इकलौती बेटी है, इसलिए उसकी शादी बड़ी धूम-धाम से की गई।
पल्लवी	तुम्हारे पास फ़ोटो तो ज़रूर होंगी। मुझे कभी दिखाना।
अलका	अच्छा, कल लाऊँगी। तुम्हारे लिए शादी की मिठाई लाई हूँ, उसके साथ।
पल्लवी	अरे, मेरी बस आ गई! अच्छा, मैं चली!
अलका	कल मिलेंगे।

1.2 Meeting friends

At the bus stop

| Alka | Hello, Pallavi! How are you? |
| Pallavi | Hello, Alka! I'm very well, but tell me, how have you been? Haven't seen you around for a while. |

Alka	Yes, I'd taken a week off from work.
Pallavi	How come? Hope all is well? Are Rahul and the children okay, too?
Alka	Oh, yes, we're all fine. My uncle's daughter was getting married, so the four of us had gone to Jaipur.
Pallavi	Oh, so it was a wedding you'd gone to. Did you enjoy it?
Alka	Yes, we had great fun. She's an only daughter, so the wedding was a grand affair.
Pallavi	You must have some photos. Do show them to me sometime.
Alka	Right, I'll get them tomorrow, along with the wedding sweets I brought along for you.
Pallavi	Hey, there's my bus! I'm off, then!
Alka	See you tomorrow.

1.3   अपना परिचय देना

सीढ़ी पर भेंट

राजन	नमस्ते। आप श्रीमती कुमार होंगी हमारे नीचे वाले मकान से।
आन्या	जी। नमस्कार।
राजन	मैं राजन जैन हूँ। आप मेरी पत्नी पल्लवी से मिल चुकी हैं। उसने आपके बारे में बताया। तो आपको यहाँ कैसा लग रहा है?
आन्या	बहुत अच्छा। गुलमोहर बाग बहुत सुन्दर और शांत मुहल्ला है। और मुझे काम पर भी दूर नहीं जाना पड़ेगा।
राजन	आप कहाँ काम करती हैं?
आन्या	माक्स म्युलर भवन में। आप शायद जानते होंगे – कस्तूरबा गांधी मार्ग पर है वह। जनवरी से मैं वहाँ जर्मन पढ़ाऊँगी।
राजन	हाँ, वह यहाँ से काफ़ी पास है। मुझे तो अस्पताल पहुँचने में सुबह कभी कभी एक धंटा लग जाता है।
आन्या	अस्पताल? तो आप डाक्टर हैं?
राजन	जी। होली फ़ैमली अस्पताल के हृदयरोग केंद्र में काम करता हूँ।
आन्या	यानी आप दिल के डाक्टर हैं।
राजन	हाँ, बस कुछ दिल के रोग ऐसे होते हैं जिनका इलाज अच्छे से अच्छा डाक्टर भी नहीं कर पाता!

आन्या जी? ओहो, मैं समझी! आप मज़ाक कर रहें हैं।इस रोग के बारे में अनगिनत बॉलीवुड फ़िल्में बनाई गई हैं न?
राजन सही है। और आपकी हिन्दी सचमुच उम्दा है!
आन्या शुक्रिया। अच्छा मुझे अब घर चलना चाहिये। फिर मिलेंगे।
राजन नमस्ते। आपसे मिलकर बहुत खुशी हुई।

1.3   Introducing oneself

An encounter on the stairs

Rajan Good evening. You must be Mrs. Kumar from the flat below ours.
Anja Yes. Good evening.
Rajan I'm Rajan Jain. You've already met my wife, Pallavi. She told me about you. So how do you like it here?
Anja It's very nice. Gulmohar Bagh is a pretty and peaceful neighbourhood. And I don't have to commute too far to work either.
Rajan Where do you work?
Anja At Max Mueller Bhavan. You might know it – it's on Kasturba Gandhi Marg. I'm going to be teaching German there from January.
Rajan Yes, that's fairly close. I sometimes need as much as an hour to get to the hospital in the morning.
Anja Hospital? So you're a doctor?
Rajan: Yes, I work in the cardiology department at Holy Family hospital.
Anja You're a heart specialist, then.
Rajan Yes, only there are some maladies of the heart which even the best doctor can't cure!
Anja Pardon? Oh, I get it – you're joking! Countless Bollywood films have been made about this sickness, haven't they?
Rajan That's right. And your Hindi really is excellent!
Anja Thank you. Well, I should be getting home now. See you later.
Rajan Bye! It was a pleasure meeting you.

1.4 किसी का परिचय देना

स्वागत अभिभाषण

प्रॉफ़ेसर दत्त हिन्दी विभाग की ओर से मैं जयप्रकाश कालिज में डाक्टर अजय कुमार का अभिनंदन करता हूँ। डा. कुमार हमारे नए प्राध्यापक हैं। दिल्ली आने से पहले आपने अमरीका और जर्मनी के विश्व–विद्यालयों में अध्ययन और अध्यापन किया। आपने हिन्दी साहित्य के अतिरिक्त जर्मन साहित्य का भी अध्ययन किया है और अनेक जर्मन कविताओं व कहानियों का हिन्दी में अनुवाद किया है। आपका हार्दिक स्वागत है, डा. कुमार!

1.4 Introducing somebody

A welcome address

Prof. Datt On behalf of the Hindi department of Jaiprakash College, I would like to extend a cordial welcome to Dr. Ajay Kumar. Dr. Kumar is our new lecturer. Before he came to Delhi, he taught and did research at universities in America and Germany. In addition to being a scholar of Hindi literature, he has also studied German literature and translated several German poems and short stories into Hindi. A very cordial welcome to you, Dr. Kumar!

शब्दावली   **Glossary**

1.1 मेहमानों का स्वागत: नए पड़ोसी
1.1 Welcoming guests: new neighbours

मेहमान *m*   a guest

स्वागत *m*   a welcome; a reception

नया   new

पड़ोसी *m*   a neighbour

नमस्ते   greetings! A common spoken
greeting or word of farewell

श्रीमती *f*   Mrs. (form of address for
married women)

कहना   to say, to speak, to tell

माफ़ कीजिये   excuse me!

पहचानना   to recognise

दूसरी मंज़िल *f*   second floor

नीचे   below, under, underneath

फ़्लैट *m*   a flat

फ़्लैट लेना   to buy/rent a flat

अंदर   within, inside

पत्नी *f*   a wife

मिलना   to meet

ख़ुशी *f*   happiness, pleasure

अरे वाह!   Bravo! Wow! Splendid!

अच्छा   good, well, fine

बोलना   to speak, to talk

लेकिन   but

भारत *m*   India

भारत की   from India

जर्मन   German

विश्वविद्यालय *m*   a university

सीखना   to learn

बढ़िया   excellent, fine

अच्छा   *interjection* Good! Well!

लेना   to take

चाय *f*   tea

कुछ   something

ठंडा/ठंढा   cold

धन्यवाद   thank you

पीना   to drink

फिर कभी   some other time

जी   an expression of respect (used
after proper names)

आज   today

लोग *pl.*   people

हम लोग   we

ज़रा   a little

जल्दी *f* में होना   to be in a hurry

सिर्फ़   only, merely

परिवार *m*   a family

सहित   along with, together with

गृह प्रवेश *m*   a house-warming
ceremony

बुलाना   to call, to invite

कल   1. tomorrow 2. yesterday

शाम *f*   the evening

सात बजे   (at) seven o'clock

पूजा *f*   a religious ceremony

खाना *m*   1. food 2. to eat *(verb)*

आप लोग   you *(plural)*

न?   *rhetorical* is it not so?

जी हाँ   *polite assent* yes, true

अवश्य   certainly, of course

आना   to come

अगर   if

किसी भी तरह का/की/के   any kind of

मदद *f*   help, aid, support

ज़रूरत *f*   need, necessity

ज़रूरत होना   to be needed

बताना   to inform, to tell

शुक्रिया *m*   thank you
ऊपर वाला *m*   situated or dwelling above, *also* God
हमेशा   always
चाहिये होना   is wanted / needful

बिलकुल   entirely, completely
ठीक   right, true
कहना   to say, to speak, to tell
चलना   to start, to depart, to set out
फिर   1. again 2. afterwards, then, next

1.2 दोस्तों से मुलाकात: बस स्टॉप पर
1.2 Meeting friends: at the bus stop

तुम कैसी हो?   how are you?
बिलकुल ठीक   very well
लेकिन   but
बताना   to inform, to tell, to describe
हाल-चाल *m*   present circumstances, condition
कई   several, a few
दिन *m*   a day; daytime
कई दिनों से   a few/several days since
दिखाई देना   to be visible, to appear
दफ़्तर *m*   an office, a workplace
हफ़्ता *m*   a week
छुट्टी *f*   a holiday/ a vacation, leave
छुट्टी लेना   to take leave or a holiday
ख़ैरियत *f*   1. well-being 2. good fortune
मज़े में   well, contented
मज़े में हूँ   things are fine with me
चाचा *m*   an uncle (father's younger brother)
लड़की *f*   a daughter, a girl
शादी *f*   marriage, a wedding

इसलिए   for this reason, therefore
चार   four
जयपुर   Jaipur (the capital of the North Indian state of Rajasthan)
मज़ा *m*   fun, enjoyment
ख़ूब मज़ा आना   to have a lot of fun, to have a good time
इकलौती बेटी *f*   an only daughter
बड़ा   1. big, great 2.very, exceedingly
धूम-धाम *f*   display, ostentation
फ़ोटो *f*   a photograph
ज़रूर   certainly, of course
कभी   sometime
दिखाना   to show
अच्छा   *interjection* well!
मिठाई *f*   a sweet
के साथ   together with, along with
अरे   *interjection* Hey! Oh!
बस *f*   a bus
कल मिलेंगे   see you tomorrow

1.3 अपना परिचय देना: सीढ़ी पर भेंट
1.3 Introducing oneself: an encounter on the stairs

नीचे   below, under, underneath
मकान *m*   a flat, a house, a dwelling
जी   *polite assent:* yes, true, very good
मिलना   to meet
चुकना   to be finished, completed
मिल चुका होना   to have met (already)
के बारे में   about, concerning
बताना   to inform, to tell, to describe
लगना   to be felt, experienced
अच्छा लगना   to be pleasing, to please
गुलमोहर बाग   Gulmohar Bagh (the
                name of a neighborhood)
सुन्दर   beautiful
शांत   quiet, tranquil, peaceful
मुहल्ला *m*   a neighbourhood, a quarter
काम *m*   work, occupation, activity
काम पर जाना   to go to work
दूर   far away, distant
पड़ना   to have to
कहाँ   where
भवन *m*   home, abode *also* a building
माक्स म्युलर भवन *m*   Max Mueller
                Bhawan (the name of the
                Goethe-Institut in India)
शायद   perhaps, maybe
मार्ग *m*   a road
जनवरी *f*   January
जर्मन   German
पढ़ाना   to teach
काफ़ी   quite, fairly
पास   nearby, near
अस्पताल *m*   a hospital
पहुँचना   to arrive, to reach
सुबह *f*   morning; in the morning

कभी कभी   sometimes
घंटा *m*   an hour
लग जाना   to take, to cost
डाक्टर *m*   a doctor
हृदयरोग *m*   heart disease
केंद *m*   a centre
यानी   that is, i.e.
दिल *m*   the heart
दिल का डाक्टर   a cardiologist,
                a heart specialist
बस   only
कुछ   some
रोग *m*   an illness, a disease
दिल का रोग   heart disease
इलाज *m*   1. a remedy, a cure
            2. treatment
इलाज करना   to treat, to cure
अच्छे से अच्छा   the very best
कर पाना   to manage to do
जी?   pardon?
ओहो   *interjection* oh!
समझना   to understand
मज़ाक *m*   a joke
अनगिनत   innumerable, countless
बॉलीवुड   Bollywood (collective term
            for commercial Hindi cinema)
फ़िल्म *f*   a film
बनाना   to make
सही   quite right, correct, exactly
सचमुच   really, truly
उम्दा   excellent
घर चलना   to set out for home
चाहिये   should
फिर मिलेंगे   see you later

1.4 किसी का परिचय देना: स्वागत अभिभाषण
1.4 Introducing somebody: a welcome address

स्वागत *m*   a welcome, a reception
अभिभाषण *m*   formal address
विभाग *m*   a department
की ओर से   on behalf of
अभिनंदन *m* करना   to greet
पाध्यापक *m*   a (university) lecturer
से पहले   before, earlier than, ahead of
आप   *honorific* he/she
अमरीका *m*   America
जर्मनी *m*   Germany

अध्ययन *m*   study, research
अध्यापन *m*   teaching
साहित्य *m*   literature
के अतिरिक्त   apart from, in addition to
अनेक   several
कविता *f*   a poem, poetry
व   and
कहानी *f*   a story
अनुवाद *m*   a translation
हार्दिक   cordial, hearty

2
यात्रा पर निकलना
Going on a trip

2.1 ऑटोरिक्शा की सवारी

 6

किराया तय करना

पल्लवी	ऑटो! ऑटो! नई दिल्ली रेलवे स्टेशन चलेंगे?
ऑटोरिक्शेवाला	बैठिए। एक सौ बीस रुपये लगेंगे।
पल्लवी	एक सौ बीस! इतना ज़्यादा क्यों?
रिक्शेवाला	ज़्यादा कहाँ है, मेमसाहब। इतना ही लगता है।
पल्लवी	तो आप मीटर चलाइए। जितना बनेगा, उतना ही दूँगी।
रिक्शेवाला	अरे, मेमसाहब, मीटर से भी इतना ही बनता है। मेरा मीटर अभी ख़राब है, चलता नहीं।

पल्लवी	यहाँ से स्टेशन के ज़्यादा से ज़्यादा नब्बे रुपये बनते हैं, यह मुझे ठीक मालूम है।
रिक्शेवाला	पहले लगते होंगे, लेकिन गैस का दाम आजकल कितना बढ़ गया है। और आपके पास सामान भी है – उसके पैसे तो अलग लगते हैं।
पल्लवी	अच्छा,अच्छा चलिए, नहीं तो बहस करने में मेरी ट्रेन ही छूट जाएगी!

2.1   An autorickshaw ride

Negotiating the fare

Pallavi	Auto! Auto! Will you take me to the New Delhi railway station?
Driver	Have a seat. It will cost you a hundred and twenty Rupees.
Pallavi	A hundred and twenty! Why so much?
Driver	It isn't too much, Ma'am. That's what it costs.
Pallavi	Well then, put the meter down. I'll pay what it shows.
Driver	Oh, come on, Ma'am, it's exactly what the meter would show. It's just that my meter isn't working right now.
Pallavi	It takes ninety rupees at the most from here to the station, I know that very well.
Driver	That might be what it used to cost, but the price of gas has risen so much these days. And besides, you have luggage – that costs extra.
Pallavi	All right, all right, let's go, or I'll miss my train while we stand here arguing!

2.2   रेलवे स्टेशन पर

7

स्टेशन पर पूछ-ताछ

कुली	बहनजी, कुली चाहिए? कौन-सी गाड़ी से जाना है?
पल्लवी	बम्बई की राजधानी एक्सप्रेस किस प्लैटफ़ौर्म से जाती है?

कुली	आम तौर पर तो दो नम्बर प्लैटफ़ौर्म से चलती है पर बम्बई की गाड़ियों में आज सब कुछ गड़बड़ है। सब देर से चल रही हैं। सामने पूछ-ताछ से पता करना पड़ेगा। लाइए, सामान दीजिए।
पल्लवी	नहीं, मुझे कुली की ज़रूरत नहीं है, सिर्फ़ यह छोटी-सी अटैची है मेरे पास।
कुली	(बड़बड़ाता हुआ) कुली चाहिए नहीं, फ़ालतू सवाल-जवाब करने लग जाते हैं लोग ...
पल्लवी	(पूछ-ताछ खिड़की पर) मुम्बई राजधानी कितने बजे छूटेगी?
रेल कर्मचारी	पाँच बजकर दस मिनट पर प्लैटफ़ौर्म नंबर ग्यारह से रवाना होगी।
पल्लवी	अरे! सवा धंटे की देरी! क्या बात हो गई है?
रेल कर्मचारी	बम्बई की लाइन पर एक दुर्घटना हो गई है इसलिए उस तरफ़ की सभी गाड़ियाँ आज देर से चल रही हैं।
पल्लवी	ओहो! तो क्या इतनी ही देर से कल सवेरे बम्बई सेंट्रल पहुँचेगी?
रेल कर्मचारी	इसके बारे में अभी कुछ नहीं कहा जा सकता है, मैडम।
पल्लवी	अच्छा, शुक्रिया।

2.2   At the railway station

Making enquiries

Porter	Need a porter, ma'am? Which train are you taking?
Pallavi	From which platform does the Rajdhani Express to Bombay leave?
Porter	It normally leaves from platform 2, but everything's all muddled up with the Bombay trains today. You'll have to find out from the enquiry counter just across. Here, let me take your luggage.
Pallavi	No, I don't need a porter, I have just this little suitcase.
Porter	(muttering) Some people start asking useless questions when they don't even need a porter ...
Pallavi	(at the enquiry window) What time is the Bombay Rajdhani leaving?
Rail employee	Departure is at ten past five from platform 11.
Pallavi	Oh! That's a delay of an hour and a quarter! What has happened?
Rail employee	There has been an accident on the Bombay line, which is why all the trains in that direction are running late today.

Pallavi	Oh dear! Will it reach Bombay Central just as late tomorrow morning?
Rail employee	It's impossible to say anything yet, Madam.
Pallavi	Okay, thanks.

2.3   रेल यात्रा

8 सहयात्री से बातचीत

पल्लवी	सुनो बेटा, यह तुम्हारी चीज़ें हैं? इनको ज़रा हटा लो, यह मेरी सीट है।
बच्चा	पापा, पापा! यह आंटी कह रही हैं कि यह सीट हमारी नहीं है, उनकी है।
सहयात्री	वह ठीक ही तो कह रही हैं, बेटे। (पल्लवी से) माफ़ कीजिएगा, चौबीस नम्बर बर्थ आपकी है?
पल्लवी	जी।
सहयात्री	क्या आप अकेले सफ़र कर रही हैं?
पल्लवी	जी हाँ। क्यों?
सहयात्री	आप को एतराज़ न हो तो हम सीट बदल सकते हैं?
पल्लवी	याने चौबीस नम्बर बर्थ आप लेना चाहते हैं?
सहयात्री	जी, आपकी बहुत मेहरबानी होगी। बात यह है कि मैं इन सब रिश्तेदारों के साथ बम्बई जा रहा हूँ। आरक्षण करते समय आठ सीटें इकट्ठा नहीं मिल पाई इसलिए एक बर्थ अगले डिब्बे में लेनी पड़ी। वह यदि आप ले लें तो हम लोग सब साथ रहेंगे।
पल्लवी	वैसे तो मुझे इसमें कोई मुश्किल नहीं है, बस आरक्षण-सुची पर यह बर्थ मेरे नाम पर है...
सहयात्री	उसकी आप चिंता मत कीजिए, टिकट-चेकर को मैं सब समझा दूँगा।
पल्लवी	ठीक है। अपना सीट और कम्पार्टमेंट का नम्बर मुझे बताइए।
सहयात्री	मैं खुद ही आपकी अटैची वहाँ तक पहुँचा देता हूँ। हम सब आपके बहुत आभारी हैं।

2.3 A train journey

A conversation with a fellow passenger

Pallavi	Listen, son, are these your things? Would you mind removing them, this is my seat.
Child	Papa, papa, the lady says this is her seat, not ours!
Rail traveller	She is quite right, my son. (To Pallavi) Excuse me, is berth number 24 yours?
Pallavi	It is.
Traveller	Are you travelling alone?
Pallavi	Yes. Why?
Traveller	If you don't mind, could we change places?
Pallavi	You mean you'd like to take berth 24?
Traveller	Yes, it would be very kind of you. The thing is that I'm travelling to Bombay with all these relatives of mine. While making reservations we didn't get eight berths together, which is why we had to take one berth in the next coach. If you took that instead, we could all be together.
Pallavi	Well, I don't really have a problem with that, it's just that on the reservation chart, this berth is in my name …
Traveller	Don't worry about that, I'll explain everything to the ticket checker.
Pallavi	All right. Tell me your seat and compartment number.
Traveller	I'll take your suitcase there myself. We're all really very grateful to you.

2.4 होटल में

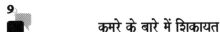

कमरे के बारे में शिकायत

पल्लवी	नमस्ते। मेरा नाम पल्लवी जैन है। मैंने टेलिफ़ोन से यहाँ एक कमरा बुक कराया था।
होटल कर्मचारी	नमस्कार, मैडम! एक मिनट... जी हाँ, श्रीमती पल्लवी जैन,... आप की तीन रात की बुकिंग है, न? एक कमरा, बुधवार तक।
पल्लवी	हाँ जी।

होटल कर्मचारी	यह फ़ार्म कृपया भर दीजिए। एक हस्ताक्षर यहाँ भी कर दीजिए। धन्यवाद। यह रही आपकी चाबी। कमरा है नम्बर एक सौ तीन, यह लड़का आपको दिखा देगा।

(नौकर से) तेजसिंह! मैडम का सामान 103 नम्बर कमरे में ले जाओ।

पल्लवी — सुबह का नाश्ता यहाँ कितने बजे मिलता है?

होटल कर्मचारी — नाश्ता आपको सवेरे साढ़े सात से साढ़े दस बजे तक हमारे रेस्तराँ ''वैशाली'' में मिलेगा जो इसी मंजिल पर है।

पल्लवी — कमरा मैं पहले देखना चाहूँगी।

होटल कर्मचारी — हाँ, ज़रूर। आप इस लड़के के साथ जाइए।

(पाँच मिनट बाद) क्या हुआ, मैडम, कमरा पसंद नहीं आया?

पल्लवी — कैसा कमरा दिया है आपने मुझे! सबसे पहले तो उसकी खिड़कियाँ ठीक सड़क के ऊपर खुलती हैं - रात-दिन शोर-गुल मचता रहेगा। इसके अलावा उसकी सही ढंग से सफ़ाई भी नहीं हुई है: गुस्ल-ख़ाने में सिंक बिलकुल गंदा है और बिस्तर पर बिछी चादर पर दाग़ पड़े हैं। आपके होटल से मुझे यह उम्मीद न थी।

होटल कर्मचारी — क्षमा चाहता हूँ, मैडम। मैं इसी समय कमरे को दुबारा साफ़ करवाता हूँ।

पल्लवी — देखिये, मुझे शांत कमरे की ज़रूरत है। अगर आप मुझे इससे बेहतर कमरा नहीं दे सकते, तो अपने मैनेजर को बुलाइए, मैं सीधे उन्हीं से शिकायत करती हूँ।

होटल कर्मचारी — नहीं, नहीं, मैडम, मुझे दो मिनट दीजिए। मैं यही देख रहा हूँ कि बग़ीचे की तरफ़ का कोई कमरा खाली है क्या। हाँ, एक है, नम्बर पाँच सौ तेरह। बहुत सुन्दर कमरा है, एकदम शांत। आपको बेशक पसंद आएगा। वैसे तो ज़रा महँगा पड़ता, लेकिन अतिरिक्त दाम हम आप से नहीं लेंगे।

पल्लवी — अच्छी बात है। नम्बर पाँच सौ तेरह भी देख लेती हूँ।

2.4   In a hotel

A complaint about the hotel room

Pallavi   Good afternoon. I'm Pallavi Jain. I had made a room reservation on the phone.

Receptionist	Good afternoon, Ma'am. Just a minute ... yes, Mrs. Pallavi Jain, ... you have a booking for three nights, is that right? One room until Wednesday.
Pallavi	That's right.
Receptionist	Please complete this form. Another signature here, please. Thank you. Here's your key. You have room 103, this boy will show it to you. (To bellboy) Tej Singh! Take the lady's luggage to room 103.
Pallavi	When is breakfast served?
Receptionist	You can get breakfast from seven thirty to ten in the morning in our restaurant 'Vaishali' which is on this floor.
Pallavi	I'd like to see the room first.
Receptionist	Certainly. Please go with the bellboy. (Five minutes later) What happened, Madam, didn't you like the room?
Pallavi	What kind of room have you given me? In the first place, the windows open right above the road – there will be a frightful din day and night. Apart from that, the room hasn't even been cleaned properly: the bathroom sink is filthy and there are stains on the bedsheet. This is not what I expected from your hotel.
Receptionist	I'm sorry, Madam. I'll get the room cleaned again immediately.
Pallavi	Look, I need a quiet room. If you can't give me a better room than this one, then please call your manager and I'll complain to him directly.
Receptionist	No, no, Madam, give me a couple of minutes. I'm just checking to see if a room looking out on the garden is free. Ah, yes, there is one – number 513. It's a very nice room, absolutely quiet. I'm sure you'll like it. It would have cost a little more, in fact, but we won't charge you the difference.
Pallavi	Fine. Let me take a look at 513 as well.

शब्दावली   **Glossary**

2.1 ऑटोरिक्शा की सवारी: किराया तय करना
2.1 An autorickshaw ride: negotiating the fare

सवारी *f*   a ride; a passenger
किराया *m*   a fare
तय करना   to decide
ऑटो *m*   an autorickshaw
रेलवे स्टेशन *m*   railway station
चलना   1. to go, to move 2. to start, to depart, to set out
रिक्शेवाला *m*   a rickshaw driver
एक सौ बीस   one hundred and twenty
रुपया *m*   rupee
लगना   to cost
ज़्यादा   much
क्यों   why
मेमसाहब *f*   *form of address* madam, lady
इतना   as much/many as this
मीटर *m*   a taxicab meter
मीटर चलाना   to turn the taximeter on

अभी   at the present moment
ख़राब   defective, damaged
यहाँ   here
ज़्यादा से ज़्यादा   at most
नब्बे   ninety
मालूम होना   to be or become known
पहले   earlier, previously, before
गैस *f*   gas
दाम *m*   a price, the cost, the rate
आजकल   nowadays, recently
कितना   how much
बढ़ना   to increase, to rise
सामान *m*   luggage
पैसा *m*   money
अलग   separately
बहस *f*   an argument/a dispute/a quarrel
ट्रेन *f*   a train
छूटना   to leave, to depart

2.2 रेलवे स्टेशन पर: स्टेशन पर पूछ-ताछ
2.2 At the railway station: making enquiries

पूछ-ताछ *f*   an enquiry
बहनजी *f*   sister; a polite form of address for a woman
कुली *m*   a porter
कौन-सी   which
गाड़ी *f*   a train; a vehicle
बम्बई *f*   Bombay / Mumbai
एक्स्प्रेस *f*   an express train
किस   which

प्लैटफ़ॉर्म *m*   a (railway) platform
आम तौर पर   usually
दो नम्बर   number two
आज   today
सब कुछ   everything
गड़बड़ *m*   disorder, confusion
देर से   late
सामने   in front, facing
पता करना   to find out

देना to give
सिर्फ़ only, merely
छोटी-सी small, little
अटैची *f* a suitcase, an attaché case
बड़बड़ाना to mutter, to grumble
फ़ालतू surplus, spare
सवाल–जवाब *m* a discussion, a debate
लोग *f* people
खिड़की a window
कितना how much?
कितने बजे at what time
पाँच five
दस ten
मिनट *m* a minute
ग्यारह eleven

रवाना होना to depart
सवा plus a quarter
घंटा *m* an hour
देरी *f* a delay, lateness
बात *f* a matter, a concern, a thing
लाइन *f* a railway line
दुर्घटना *f* an accident
तरफ़ *f* side, direction
सवेरा *m* the morning
सवेरे in the morning
बम्बई सेंट्रल *m* Bombay Central railway
station
कुछ नहीं nothing
कहना to say, to speak, to tell

2.3 रेल यात्रा: सहयात्री से बातचीत
2.3 A train journey: a conversation with a fellow passenger

सुनना to hear
बेटा *m* 1. a son 2. a form of address
used by adults for children
चीज़ *f* a thing
ज़रा just; would you mind, please?
सीट *f* a seat
आंटी *f* aunty; a form of address used
by children to show respect to
(unrelated) women
ठीक right, true
चौबीस twenty four
बर्थ *f* a berth on a train
अकेले alone, on one's own
सफ़र *m* a journey; travelling
क्यों why
एतराज़ *m* an objection
बदलना to exchange

सकना to be able
याने that is
लेना to take
मेहरबानी *f* kindness
रिश्तेदार *m, pl* a relative
आरक्षण *m* a reservation (of a seat)
समय *m* the time
आठ eight
इकट्ठा together
अगला next, following
डिब्बा *m* a railway carriage/
compartment
साथ together
वैसे तो on the whole, in fact
मुश्किल *f* a difficulty
बस only, merely
आरक्षण–सूची *f* a reservation chart/list

चिंता *f*   concern, anxiety, worry
टिकट-चेकर *m*   a ticket inspector/ checker
समझाना   to explain

कंपार्टमेंट *m*   compartment in a train
पहुँचाना   1. to escort 2. to deliver
आभारी   grateful, obliged

2.4 होटल में: कमरे के बारे में शिकायत
2.4 In a hotel: a complaint about the hotel room

होटल *m*   a hotel
कमरा *m*   a room
के बारे में   about, concerning
शिकायत *f*   a complaint
टेलीफ़ोन *m*   a telephone
बुक करना   to reserve, to book
मिनट *m*   a minute
तीन   three
रात *f*   a night
बुकिंग *f*   a booking
बुधवार *m*   Wednesday
तक   until
फ़ार्म *m*   a form
कृपया / कृपा *f* करके   kindly, please
भरना   to fill (up)
हस्ताक्षर *m*   a signature
चाबी *f*   a key
एक सौ तीन   one hundred and three
लड़का *m*   a boy
दिखाना   to show
नौकर *m*   a servant, an attendant
सुबह *f*   morning; in the morning
नाश्ता *m*   breakfast
मिलना   to be available
सवेरा *m*   the morning
साढ़े   plus a half
साढ़े सात (बजे)   half past seven
साढ़े दस (बजे)   half past ten
रेस्तराँ / रेस्तोराँ / रेस्टोरेंट *m*   a restaurant

मंज़िल *f*   a storey, a floor (of a building)
देखना   to see, to inspect
चाहना   to wish, to ask for, to choose
के साथ   together with, along with
बाद   after
पसंद आना   to please, to be liked (by)
पहले   first
सबसे पहले   in the first place, firstly
खिड़की *f*   a window
सड़क *f*   a road
के ऊपर   over, above
खुलना   to be open(ed)
रात-दिन   day and night
शोर-गुल *m*   noise, a din, a racket
मचना   to be caused, to be produced
के अलावा   1. in addition 2. apart from
सही   correct
ढंग *m*   a way, a manner, a method
सफ़ाई *f*   cleanliness
सफ़ाई करना   to clean, to tidy
गुस्ल-ख़ाना *m*   a bathroom
सिंक *m*   a washbasin
बिलकुल   entirely, completely
गंदा   dirty, filthy
बिस्तर *m*   a bed, bedclothes
बिछना   to be spread out
चादर *f*   a sheet
दाग़ *m*   a spot, a stain
उम्मीद *f*   hope, expectation

क्षमा *f* forgiveness, pardon

दुबारा repeated, a second time

साफ़ clean

करवाना to have or to get done

शांत quiet, tranquil, peaceful

मैनेजर *m* a manager

बुलाना to call, to summon, to send for

सीधे directly

बग़ीचा / बाग़ीचा *m* a garden

ख़ाली empty, free

पाँच सौ तेरह five hundred and thirteen

सुन्दर beautiful

बेशक undoubtedly, certainly

वैसे तो in fact

ज़रा a little

महँगा expensive

अतिरिक्त extra

दाम *m* a price, the rate

3
शहर में घूमना–फिरना
Travelling around the city

3.1   दर्शनीय स्थानों की सैर

दिल्ली दर्शन की तैयारी

अजय	इस शनिवार को मैं आन्या को दिल्ली के कुछ दर्शनीय स्थल दिखाना चाहता हूँ। मैं सोच रहा हूँ कि शायद हम लोगों को एक दिन के लिए किराए पर गाड़ी ले लेनी चाहिए।
आन्या	अरे नहीं, अजय, यहाँ दिल्ली की भीड़–भाड़ में गाड़ी कौन चलाएगा!
राजन	निश्चिंत रहिए, आन्या जी! इस देश में गाड़ी के साथ चालक भी मिलता है। किराये में गाड़ी और ड्राइवर दोनों ही शामिल होते हैं।
पल्लवी	कोने के टैक्सी–स्टैंड से आपको पूरे दिन की टैक्सी मिल जाएगी। वहाँ के ड्राइवर भी अच्छे हैं और किराया भी उचित होता है।

राजन	तो कहाँ–कहाँ जाने का इरादा है?
आन्या	मैंने सुना है कि राष्ट्रीय संग्रहालय में लघु-चित्रों का बहुत सुन्दर संकलन है। उसे देखने को मैं बहुत उत्सुक हूँ।
पल्लवी	चित्र-कला ही नहीं, राष्ट्रीय संग्रहालय की मूर्ति-कला भी शानदार है। वह सचमुच देखने लायक है।
अजय	इस के अलावा हम लोग हुमायूँ का मक़बरा भी देखना चाहते हैं। और समय होने पर पुरानी दिल्ली जाकर जामा मस्जिद और लाल क़िला भी।
आन्या	उसके बाद रात का ख़ाना हम बाहर ही खाना चाहते हैं। क्या आप लोग कोई होटल बता सकते हैं जिसमें लज़ीज़ भारतीय व्यंजन मिलें?
पल्लवी	आपको भारत की रसोई पसंद है, आन्या? तो क्यों न हम लोग साथ ख़ाने चलें? राजन और मैं भी शनिवार की रात को रेस्तराँ जा रहे हैं। वह आज़ाद नगर में है, यहाँ से ज़्यादा दूर नहीं।
राजन	यह रेस्तराँ नया खुला है और पल्लवी ने उसकी इतनी तारीफ़ सुनी है कि हम उसे ख़ुद परखना चाहते हैं।
आन्या	यह तो बहुत बढ़िया सुझाव है!
अजय	हाँ, हाँ, क्यों नहीं! होटल का नाम और पता हमें दे दीजिएगा।

3.1   Sightseeing

Preparing for a tour of Delhi

Ajay	I want to show Anja some of the sights of Delhi this Saturday. I'm wondering if we should hire a car for the day.
Anja	Oh, no, Ajay, who wants to drive on these crowded Delhi roads!
Rajan	Don't worry, Anja-ji! In this country you hire a driver along with the car. The car and the driver are both included in the fare.
Pallavi	You can hire a taxi for a whole day from the taxi-stand at the corner. Their drivers are good and their charges are fair as well.
Rajan	So which places do you plan to visit?
Anja	I've heard that the National Museum has a very beautiful collection of miniatures. I'm really keen to see it.

Pallavi	It's not only the paintings, the National Museum's collection of sculpture is also superb. It's really worth seeing.
Ajay	Apart from that, we also want to see Humayun's tomb. And, if we have the time, then we'd like to go to Old Delhi and see the Jama Masjid and the Red Fort as well.
Anja	After that we'd like to go out for dinner. Could you recommend a restaurant that serves delicious Indian dishes?
Pallavi	Do you like Indian cooking, Anja? Why don't we go out for a meal together, then? Rajan and I are also going to a restaurant on Saturday night. It's in Azad Nagar, not too far from here.
Rajan	This restaurant has opened recently and Pallavi has heard such praise of it that we wanted to try it out ourselves.
Anja	That's an excellent idea!
Ajay	Yes, indeed! Please give us the name and address of the restaurant.

3.2　　दर्शनीय स्थल

10

राष्ट्रीय संग्रहालय की टिकट खिड़की पर

अजय	मुझे दो प्रवेश-टिकट दीजिएगा।
कार्यकर्ता	आप के साथ जो महिला हैं, वे विदेशी नागरिक हैं न? उनके टिकट के डेढ़ सौ रुपये लगेंगे। भारतीय नागरिकों के लिए प्रवेश शुल्क केवल दस रुपये है।
अजय	यह देशी और परदेशी के लिए अलग-अलग दाम कब से वसूल किये जाते हैं? पहले तो सबके लिए एक ही शुल्क हुआ करता था।
कार्यकर्ता	शुल्क में परिवर्तन के तो पाँच-छः वर्ष हो चुके हैं। भारतीय पुरातत्व सर्वेक्षण के आदेश के अनुसार भारत के सभी स्मारकों का प्रवेश शुल्क बदला गया है। देखिए, इस सूचना-पट्ट पर यह सब लिखा हुआ है।
आन्या	ओह, कैमरा शुल्क में भी अंतर है!
कार्यकर्ता	जी हाँ, भारतीय दर्शकों को संग्रहालय में कैमरा ले जाने के लिए बीस रुपये देने पड़ते है, और अन्य दर्शकों को तीन सौ रुपये। क्या आपके पास कैमरा है, मैडम?

आन्या	जी ... मेरा मतलब है, नहीं, नहीं! यह कैमरा तो मेरे पति का है, कम से कम आज के लिये। इस पर आप भारतीय शुल्क ही लगाइये। यह लो अजय, अपना कैमरा संभालो।
कार्यकर्ता	कोई बात नहीं, मैडम, आप कैमरा अपने पास रख सकती हैं। आपके कुल मिलाकर एक सौ अस्सी रुपये बने।
अजय	क्या यहाँ संग्रहालय के पोस्टकार्ड भी मिलते हैं?
कार्यकर्ता	हाँ, हाँ, हमारे पास संकलन की अनेक कलाकृतियों के पोस्टकार्ड भी हैं और अनुकृतियाँ भी। यह देखिए। ये पोस्टकार्ड बीस–बीस रुपये के हैं।
आन्या	बहुत सुन्दर हैं। यह छह पोस्टकार्ड हमें दे दीजिए।
कार्यकर्ता	अवश्य। और कुछ? नहीं? तो आप के तीन सौ रुपये हुए।

3.2   Sightseeing attractions

At the National Museum ticket counter

Ajay	I'd like two entry tickets, please.
Official	The lady accompanying you is a foreign national, isn't she? Her ticket will cost 150 rupees. For Indian nationals, the entry fee is just 10 rupees.
Ajay	Since when are different prices being charged from nationals and foreigners? There used to be just one price for everybody before.
Official	It has been five or six years since the change in rates. The entry fee for all monuments in India has been revised in accordance with a directive from the Archeological Survey of India. Look, it is all written here on this notice board.
Anja	Oh, there is a difference in the camera charges as well!
Official	Yes, Indian visitors have to pay 20 rupees to take a camera into the museum, and other visitors pay 300 rupees. Do you have a camera, Madam?
Anja	Yes ... I mean, no, no! This camera is my husband's, at least for today. Please charge the Indian price for it. Here, Ajay, you look after your camera.
Official	Never mind, Madam, you can keep your camera with you. That makes a total of 180 rupees.
Ajay	Are museum postcards also available here?

Official	Yes, we have postcards of several works of art in the collection and some prints as well. Here, take a look. These postcards are 20 rupees each.
Anja	Very pretty! Please give us these six postcards.
Official	Certainly. Anything else? No? That makes 300 rupees.

3.3   डाक-ख़ाने में

11 विदेश में पत्र भेजना

आन्या	अजय, यहाँ आस-पास कोई डाक-घर है क्या? हम लोग इन पोस्टकार्ड पर टिकट लगा कर इन्हें आज ही जर्मनी भेज देते हैं। मुझे एक पत्र भी डालना है।
अजय	अगर मुझे ठीक याद है तो इसी सड़क पर थोड़ी दूर आगे जाकर एक डाक-ख़ाना पड़ता है। हाँ, देखो, वह है कोने पर। चलो!
आन्या	(डाक-टिकट की खिड़की पर) सुनिए, जर्मनी के लिए पोस्टकार्ड पर कितने का टिकट लगता है?
डाक कर्मचारी	हवाई डाक से भेजना है कि समुद्री डाक से?
आन्या	हवाई डाक से। मुझे छह टिकट चाहिए।
डाक कर्मचारी	आठ रुपये का टिकट लगेगा। यह लीजिए आठ-आठ रुपये के छह टिकट।
आन्या	और इस इंग्लैंड की चिट्ठी का क्या लगेगा?
डाक कर्मचारी	चिट्ठी पर वज़न के मुताबिक़ टिकट लगता है। अपना पत्र मुझे दीजिए, इसको तौलना होगा। इसका वज़न बीस ग्राम से कम है, पंद्रह रुपये का टिकट लगाइए। एक टिकट दूँ?
आन्या	आप मुझे दस टिकट दे दीजिए पंद्रह रुपये के। हवाई डाक की चिप्पी भी मैं आप से ख़रीद सकती हूँ?
डाक कर्मचारी	हवाई डाक की चिप्पियाँ ख़रीदने की ज़रूरत नहीं होती, वे तो डाक विभाग से मुफ़्त में मिलती हैं। लेकिन मेरे पास अभी ख़तम हो गई हैं। आपको बग़ल वाले काउंटर पर मिलेंगी। यह रहे आपके टिकट और छुट्टे पैसे।
आन्या	शुक्रिया।

3.3   At the post office

Sending a letter overseas

Anja	Ajay, is there a post office somewhere close by? Let's put stamps on these postcards and send them to Germany today. I want to post a letter too.
Ajay	If I remember correctly, there's a post office a little further down the road. Yes, look, there it is at the corner. Let's go!
Anja	(at the postage stamps counter) Excuse me, how much postage is required for a postcard to Germany?
Postal clerk	Do you want to send it by air mail or by surface mail?
Anja	By air mail. I need six stamps.
Postal clerk	You'll need a stamp of eight rupees. Here you are, six stamps of eight rupees each.
Anja	And how much for this letter to England?
Postal clerk	The postage depends on the weight of the letter. Please give me your letter; it needs to be weighed. It weighs less than 20 grammes, so you'll need a stamp worth 15 rupees. Should I give you a stamp?
Anja	Please give me ten of those 15-rupee stamps. Can I also buy air mail stickers here?
Postal clerk	You don't need to buy air mail stickers, they are available free of cost from the postal department. But I don't have any right now. You'll get them at the next counter. Here are your tickets and your change.
Anja	Thank you.

3.4   रास्ता पूछना

रेस्तराँ का रास्ता पूछना

राजन	आज़ाद नगर मार्केट तो हम लोग पहुँच गए, पल्लवी। अब अपने नए रेस्तराँ का रास्ता बताओ।
पल्लवी	यहीं कहीं होना चाहिए। मैंने भी कभी देखा नहीं है, इसलिए ढूंढना पड़ेगा। ऐसा करो कि मुझे यहीं उतार दो, मैं किसी से पूछती हूँ।

राजन	ठीक है, मैं गाड़ी वहाँ सामने खड़ी करता हूँ।
पल्लवी	(राह-चलती महिला से) माफ़ कीजिएगा, आप को पता होगा कि मल्लिका रेस्तराँ कहाँ है?
महिला	मल्लिका? हाँ, उसे जानती तो हूँ लेकिन यहाँ नहीं है वह।
पल्लवी	आपको पक्का मालूम है? मुझसे तो आज़ाद नगर मार्केट कहा गया था।
महिला	लेकिन आज़ाद नगर मार्केट के दो हिस्से हैं। मल्लिका इधर नहीं, बल्कि बाज़ार के दूसरे हिस्से में है, दस ब्लॉक में। नया रेस्तराँ है न?
पल्लवी	जी हाँ, बिलकुल नया है – उसके खुले हुए अभी दो हफ़्ते भी नहीं हुए। हम कैसे पहुँचेंगे वहाँ?
महिला	आपको गाड़ी घुमा कर गोल-चक्कर तक वापस जाना पड़ेगा। गोल चक्कर पर पहली सड़क छोड़ कर दूसरी वाली पर बाएँ मुड़िएगा। उसी सड़क पर सीधे जाइएगा तो दाहिनी ओर एक छोटा-सा पार्क आएगा जिसके इर्द-गिर्द दुकानें हैं। वही है आज़ाद नगर का दूसरा बाज़ार। मल्लिका होटल बायीं तरफ़ पर है, आपको दिखाई दे जाएगा।
पल्लवी	यहाँ से कितनी दूर होगा?
महिला	नज़दीक ही है, तकरीबन एक-डेढ़ किलोमीटर। गाड़ी में आप पाँच-दस मिनट में वहाँ पहुँच जाएँगी।
पल्लवी	आपका बहुत धन्यवाद।

3.4   Asking for directions

Asking the way to a restaurant

Rajan	Well, we've got to the Azad Nagar market, Pallavi. Now tell me how to get to your new restaurant.
Pallavi	It should be somewhere here. I've never seen it before myself, so we'll have to look for it. Tell you what: let me out here, and I'll ask somebody.
Rajan	Okay, I'll park the car there across the road.
Pallavi	(To a woman passing by) Excuse me, would you know where Mallika restaurant is?
Woman	Mallika? Yes, I know it, but it isn't here.

Pallavi	Are you sure? Because Azad Nagar market is what I was told.
Woman	But Azad Nagar market has two parts. Mallika is not here, it's in the other part, in block 10. It's a new restaurant, isn't it?
Pallavi	Yes, absolutely new – it has been barely two weeks since it opened. How will we get there?
Woman	You'll have to turn the car around and go back to the roundabout. Leave the first road at the roundabout and take the second left. Go straight along this road until you get to a small park with shops around it. That's the second part of Azad Nagar market. You'll see the restaurant Mallika on the left.
Pallavi	How far is it from here approximately?
Woman	It's fairly close, about a kilometre or one and a half. You'll get there in ten or fifteen minutes by car.
Pallavi	Thank you very much.

शब्दावली   Glossary

3.1 दर्शनीय स्थानों की सैर: दिल्ली दर्शन की तैयारी
3.1 Sightseeing: preparing for a tour of Delhi

शहर *m* a city, a town
घूमना-फिरना to roam, to tour
दर्शनीय worth seeing, picturesque
स्थान *m* a place, a spot
सैर *f* an outing, a tour, a trip
तैयारी *f* preparation(s)
शनिवार *m* Saturday
कुछ some
दिख्वाना to show
सोचना to think, to reflect
शायद perhaps, maybe
किराए पर लेना to take on rent/hire
भीड़-भाड़ *m* hustle and bustle, crowds
कौन who
गाड़ी *f* चलाना to drive a car
निश्चिंत free from worry, unperturbed
देश *m* a country
चालक *m* a driver
मिलना to be found; available
ड्राइवर *m* a driver
शामिल included
कोना *m* a corner
टैक्सी-स्टैंड *m* a taxi stand
पूरा whole, complete
उचित appropriate, fitting
इरादा *m* an intention, a desire
राष्ट्रीय national
संग्रहालय *m* a museum
लघु-चित्र *m* a miniature (painting)
संकलन *m* a collection

उत्सुक eager, keen
चित्र-कला *f* painting
मूर्ति-कला *f* sculpture
शानदार magnificent
सचमुच really, truly
देखने लायक worth seeing
(के)अलावा 1. in addition to 2. apart
            from
मकबरा *m* a tomb, a mausoleum
पुराना old, of long standing
मस्जिद *m* a mosque
किला *m* a fort, a castle
(के) बाद after
रात *f* the night, night-time
रात का खाना *m* dinner
बाहर out, outside
होटल *m* a hotel, *also* a restaurant
बताना to inform, to tell, to describe
लज़ीज़ delicious, delightful
व्यंजन *m* a dish
रसोई *f* food, cuisine
पसंद होना to please, to be liked (by)
रेस्तराँ *m* a restaurant
नया new
खुलना to be open(ed)
तारीफ़ *f* praise
ख़ुद self (myself, himself, itself, etc.)
परखना to judge, to test
सुझाव *m* a suggestion
पता *m* an address

3.2 दर्शनीय स्थल: राष्ट्रीय संग्रहालय की खिड़की पर
3.2 Sightseeing attractions: at the National Museum ticket counter

स्थल *m* a place
टिकट *m* a ticket
खिड़की *f* a window
कार्यकर्ता *m* a worker, an official
प्रवेश *m* entry, admission
  प्रवेश-टिकट *m* an entry ticket
महिला *f* a woman
विदेशी foreign
नागरिक *m* citizen
डेढ़ one and a half
भारतीय Indian
शुल्क *m* a fee (as for entrance)
केवल only
देशी national, indigenous, internal
परदेशी *m* a foreigner
अलग-अलग different
वसूल करना to collect
पहले before, previously, earlier
परिवर्तन *m* a change, a transformation
वर्ष *m* a year
पुरातत्व *m* archaeology
सर्वेक्षण *m* a survey
आदेश *m* an order, a directive

(के) अनुसार according (to), following
स्मारक *m* a memorial, a monument
बदलना to change
सूचना-पट्ट *m* a signboard/ notice board
कैमरा *m* a camera
अंतर *m* a difference
दर्शक *m* a viewer
अन्य other, different
मतलब *m* a purpose/a meaning, sense
पति *m* a husband
कम से कम at least
आज today
संभालना 1. to take care of, to look after
          2. to hold, not to let go
बात *f* a matter, a topic, a concern
कोई बात नहीं no matter; that's all right
कुल entire, the whole, total
कुल मिलाकर altogether
पोस्टकार्ड *m* a postcard
अनेक several
कलाकृति *f* a work of art
अनुकृति *f* a replica
अवश्य certainly, of course

3.3 डाक-ख़ाने में: विदेश में पत्र भेजना
3.3 At the post office: sending a letter overseas

डाक-ख़ाना *m* a post office
आस-पास in the vicinity, round about
डाक-घर *m* a post office
(डाक-)टिकट *m* a postage stamp
पत्र *m* a letter
डालना to put (in a post box)

(को) याद होना to be remembered/
          recollected (by)
सड़क *f* a road
थोड़ा a little
आगे in front, ahead
पड़ना to be found/located

कर्मचारी *m* an employee, a worker
समुद्री डाक *f* surface mail
इंग्लैंड *m* England
चिट्ठी *f* a letter
वज़न *m* weight
(के) मुताबिक according (to)
तौलना to weigh
ग्राम a gramme
कम less
चिप्पी *f* a sticker

हवाई डाक *f* airmail
ख़रीदना to buy
ज़रूरत *f* need, necessity
विभाग *m* a department
मुफ़्त free, gratis
ख़तम होना to finish; to be finished
इकट्ठा (taken) together
बग़ल (में) adjoining, nearby
काउंटर *m* a sales counter/cash desk
छुट्टे (पैसे) *pl* small change

3.4 रास्ता पूछना: रेस्तराँ का रास्ता पूछना
3.4 Asking for directions: asking the way to a restaurant

मार्केट, बाज़ार *m* market
रास्ता *m* the way, a route
पूछना to ask, to enquire of
कहीं somewhere, anywhere
कभी sometime
 कभी नहीं never
ढूँढना to look for, to search (out)
ऐसा of this sort, like this
ऐसा करो (I'll) tell you what (*offering a suggestion*)
उतारना to set down/drop off
(गाड़ी) ख़ड़ी करना to park
राह-चलता *m* a passerby
महिला *f* a woman
पता होना to know, to be informed
जानना to know
पक्का definitely, surely
हिस्सा *m* a part
इधर here, over here
बल्कि but rather

ब्लॉक *m* block, area in a neighbourhood
हफ़्ता *m* a week
घुमाना to turn (something)
गोल चक्कर *m* a roundabout, a traffic circle
वापस back
दूसरा second, next
बाएँ to the left
मुड़ना to turn
सीधा straight, direct
सीधे जाना to go straight (ahead)
दाहिना right (hand)
 दाहिनी ओर right hand, on the right
पार्क *m* a park
इर्द-गिर्द all around
बायीं तरफ़ (on the) left side
दिखाई देना to be visible, to appear
नज़दीक near, close
तकरीबन approximately, about
डेढ़ one and a half
किलोमीटर a kilometre

4
खाना–पीना
Food and drink

4.1 'मल्लिका' होटल में खाना

13

खाना मंगवाना

पल्लवी	आप लोगों ने मेनू देख लिया? कुछ पसंद किया?
आन्या	इतने प्रकार के पकवानों में से एक चुनना कोई आसान काम नहीं है।
पल्लवी	तो मिल कर छह–सात चीज़ें मँगवाई जाएँ?
अजय	मेरे ख़याल से यही सबसे अच्छा रहेगा।
राजन	जी हाँ, ऐसा करने से हम सभी तरह-तरह के व्यंजन चख पाएँगे। हम लोग आम तौर पर भारतीय खाना ऐसे ही आर्डर करते हैं।
आन्या	मेरे लिए आप लोग ही पसंद कीजिए। मैं गोश्त के सिवा सब कुछ खाती हूँ।

पल्लवी	अरे वाह, तो आप मेरी तरह शाकाहारी हैं! आपको पनीर अच्छा लगता है?
आन्या	जी हाँ, बहुत अच्छा लगता है।
पल्लवी	फिर एक पालक–पनीर मँगवाते हैं। सब्ज़ियाँ और कई हैं: मसालेवाली भिंडी, आलू गोभी, शिमला–मिर्च ...
अजय	यह भरवाँ शिमला–मिर्च मज़ेदार मालूम होती है। इसे मँगाकर देखें?
राजन	हाँ, लेकिन कोई रसेदार सब्ज़ी भी होनी चाहिए, या फिर कोई दाल ... दाल मक्खनी कैसी रहेगी?
आन्या	हाँ, यह लेते हैं। यह तो मेरी मनपसंद दाल है!
पल्लवी	एक रायता भी मँगाते हैं। ख़ीरे का रायता ठीक रहेगा सबके लिए?
राजन	हाँ, रायता, दाल, तरकारी तो सब ठीक है, लेकिन हम बेचारे माँस–मछली ख़ानेवालों के मतलब की बात भी तो होनी चाहिए! अजय जी, क्या लिया जाए, तंदूर से कुछ व्यंजन या कोई शोरबेदार पाक?
अजय	दोनों ही लेकर देखें। तंदूर से मुर्ग टिक्का?
राजन	हाँ, अच्छा रहेगा। और मेनू में उसी के नीचे यह जो अदरकी दहीवाला गोश्त है, उसे ख़ाकर देखा जाए? काफ़ी है, न? तो हमारा आर्डर अब पूरा हो गया, बैरा को बुलाता हूँ।
पल्लवी	अरे रुको, राजन, रोटी और चावल तो हम लोग भूल ही गए! सादा चावल लें कि पुलाव?
आन्या	सादा चावल ही मँगवाइए। यहाँ नान नहीं मिलती क्या?
राजन	हाँ, हाँ, बेशक मिलती है। मेनू के आख़िरी पन्ने पर देखिए हर तरह की नान और रोटियाँ हैं।
पल्लवी	हमें एक 'मल्लिका रोटी की टोकरी' लेनी चाहिए। इस में नान, रोटी, पराठा सब हैं — सात अलग–अलग तरह के।
राजन	ठीक है। अब पूरा ख़ाना हो गया हो तो मँगवाया जाए। बैरा!

4.1   Eating at 'Mallika' restaurant

Ordering a meal

Pallavi	Have you had a look at the menu? Have you chosen anything?
Anja	It isn't easy to choose one dish from such a great variety.
Pallavi	So should we order six or seven things for all of us to share?

Ajay	I think that would be best.
Rajan	Yes, this way we will all be able to try out different preparations. This is how we usually order Indian food.
Anja	Please choose for me, too. I eat everything except meat.
Pallavi	Oh, good, you are a vegetarian like me! Do you like cottage cheese?
Anja	Yes, I like it very much.
Pallavi	Then let's order some spinach with cottage cheese. There are quite a few vegetable preparations: spicy okra, potatoes with cauliflower, peppers ...
Ajay	The stuffed pepper seems interesting. Should we order it and see?
Rajan	Yes, but we should also have some vegetables in a gravy, or else a lentil dish ... how about this spicy black lentil curry?
Anja	Yes, let's take that. It's my favourite lentil dish.
Pallavi	Let's order some yoghurt salad as well. Is yoghurt with cucumber okay for everyone?
Rajan	Yes, yes, yoghurt, lentils, vegetables are all very well, but there should be something of interest for us poor carnivores as well. Ajay-ji, what should we take – preparations from the clay oven or something in a gravy?
Ajay	Let's try both. Grilled chicken fillets from the clay oven?
Rajan	Yes, that's good. And this lamb in ginger and yoghurt right below it on the menu, should we try that? That'll do, won't it? So now our order is now complete. I'll call the waiter.
Pallavi	Hey, wait, Rajan, we forgot the bread and rice completely! Should we take plain boiled rice or fried rice?
Anja	Please order just the plain rice. Don't they have any nan bread here?
Rajan	Yes, they certainly do. Look, there are all kinds of breads on the last page of the menu.
Pallavi	We should order a 'Mallika bread basket'. It has seven different kinds of bread – leavened, unleavened, fried – everything.
Rajan	Fine. Now, if we've got a meal together, let's order. Waiter!

4.2 होटल में

14

खाने के पैसे चुकाना

बैरा	आप लोगों को खाना पसंद आया?
पल्लवी	जी हाँ। बहुत स्वादिष्ट था।
राजन	हर एक व्यंजन का ज़ायका उम्दा था।
बैरा	मेमसहाब के लिए मिर्च ज़्यादा तो नहीं थी?
आन्या	नहीं, बिलकुल नहीं। सब चीज़ें लज़ीज़ थीं।
बैरा	धन्यवाद। अब कुछ मीठा लेंगें? खीर, श्रीखंड, कुल्फ़ी? पिसता कुल्फ़ी हमारे होटल की ख़ासियत है।
आन्या	मेरा पेट बिलकुल भर गया है। अब बस।
पल्लवी	मुझसे भी अब और कुछ नहीं खाया जाएगा। खा–खाकर पेट फट रहा है।
राजन	खाना इतना ज़ायकेदार था कि हम सब ने कुछ ज़्यादा ही खा लिया है। आप अब बिल ले आइए। आप लोग क्रेडिट–कार्ड लेते हैं, न?
बैरा	जी, साहब। वीज़ा और मास्टर कार्ड लेते हैं। मैं बिल अभी लाया।
आन्या	अरे नहीं, राजन जी, ऐसा क्यों? बिल अकेले आप थोड़े ही देंगे!
पल्लवी	आन्या जी, हम लोगों में बाँट कर बिल चुकाने का रिवाज नहीं है।
अजय	यह आपने बिलकुल ठीक कहा, पल्लवी जी! इसी लिए प्रथानुसार में इसे चुकाने वाला हूँ। बैरा, बिल मुझे देना!
राजन	देखिए अजय, यह तो हमारी परंपरा है कि खाना खिलाने का ज़िम्मा उम्र में सबसे बड़े का होता है।
अजय	हरगिज़ नहीं! इससे मैं बिलकुल सहमत नहीं हूँ। वैसे भी परंपराओं का अंधा–धुंध पालन करना अच्छा नहीं होता।
पल्लवी	अच्छा, ऐसा करते हैं: इस बार आप लोग हमारे मेहमान हैं लेकिन अगली बार खाना आप खिलाइएगा।
आन्या	ठीक है, ऐसा ही करेंगे। आज के स्वादिष्ट खाने के लिए धन्यवाद।
अजय	और अगली बार खाने का बुलावा हमारा रहा – यह भूलिएगा मत!

4.2   In a restaurant

Paying for the meal

Waiter	Did you like the food?
Pallavi	Yes. It was delicious.
Rajan	Every single dish tasted excellent.
Waiter	Not too spicy for Madam, I hope?
Anja	No, not at all. Everything was delicious.
Waiter	Thank you. Would you like a dessert now? Rice pudding, yoghurt pudding, ice cream? The pistachio ice cream is a speciality of our restaurant.
Anja	I am absolutely full. Nothing more for me now.
Pallavi	I couldn't manage another bite either. I've eaten so much that my stomach is full to bursting.
Rajan	The food was so tasty that we've all overeaten. Please bring the bill now. You accept credit cards here, don't you?
Kellner	Yes, sir. We take Visa and Mastercard. I'll get your bill right away.
Anja	Oh, no, Rajan-ji, what's this? Surely you're not going to foot the bill alone!
Pallavi	Anja-ji, we don't follow the practice of splitting the bill here.
Ajay	Rightly said, Pallavi-ji! Which is why, in accordance with the custom, I'm going to pay. Waiter, bring me the bill!
Rajan	Look, Ajay, it is after all our tradition that the eldest bears the responsibility of providing for meals.
Ajay	Absolutely not! I don't agree with that at all. In any case, it's not good to adhere blindly to traditions.
Pallavi	All right, then, what we can do is this: this time you are our guests, but the next time, you can invite us.
Anja	Fine, that's what we'll do. Thank you for the delicious meal today.
Ajay	And next time, the invitation will be ours – don't forget that!

४.३   मिठाइयाँ

मिठाई की दुकान में

अलका	यह पीली वाली बरफ़ी किस चीज़ से बनी है?
हलवाई	यह खोए की बरफ़ी है, इसमें केसर पड़ा है।
अलका	और इसके बगल में कलाकंद है?
हलवाई	जी हाँ। कितना दूँ?
अलका	मुझे एक किलो मिली–जुली मिठाइयाँ चाहिए, लेकिन केवल ऐसी जो कुछ दिन चलें। खोए और पनीर की मिठाइयाँ तो दो–तीन दिन में ही ख़राब हो जाती हैं, न?
हलवाई	तो आप इस तरफ़ से मेवे वाली मिठाइयाँ लीजिए। यह आराम से दो हफ़्ते तक चलती हैं।।
अलका	यह बादाम बरफ़ी ताज़ी है?
हलवाई	हमारी सभी मिठाइयाँ ताज़ी होती हैं, बहनजी। आप बरफ़ी चख कर देखिए।
अलका	हाँ, यह तो वास्तव में बहुत अच्छी है। क्या हिसाब है यह?
मिठाईवाला	तीन सौ अस्सी रुपये किलो।
अलका	ठीक है, आप मेरे लिए एक किलो के डिब्बे में अंजीर रोल, काजू कतली और बादाम बरफ़ी रख कर उपहार की तरह पैक कर दीजिए।
हलवाई	और क्या लेंगी?
अलका	हाँ, एक पाव बेसन के लड्डू और पाँच रसगुल्ले भी दीजिएगा। रसगुल्ले संभाल कर पैक कीजिएगा, कहीं शीरा चुए न।
हलवाई	जी ज़रूर, रसगुल्ले कुल्हड़ में ठीक से बांध कर देंगे।
अलका	आपकी दुकान में समोसे नहीं मिलते?
हलवाई	मिलते तो हैं, लेकिन अभी तैयार नहीं हैं। समोसे बनाना हम शाम के चार बजे शुरू करते हैं। कोई और नमकीन लेंगी?
अलका	धन्यवाद, आज के लिए इतना ही काफ़ी है। मेरा हिसाब कर दीजिए।

4.3   Indian sweets

In a sweet shop

Alka	What is this yellow barfi made of?
Confectioner	It's made of thickenend milk and there is saffon in it.
Alka	And is that *kalakand* next to it?
Confectioner	Yes, it is. How much would you like?
Alka	I'd like a kilo of mixed sweets, but only those that keep a few days. The milk and cottage cheese sweets spoil in just two or three days, don't they?
Confectioner	Then you should take the sweets made from dried fruits on this side. They'll keep easily for up to two weeks.
Alka	Is this almond paste sweet fresh?
Confectioner	All our sweets are always fresh, ma'am. Here, taste this and see for yourself.
Alka	Yes, it is indeed very good. How much does it cost?
Confectioner	Three hundred eighty rupees per kilo.
Alka	Right, could you pack these fig rolls, cashewnut sweets and almond paste squares in a one-kilo box and gift wrap it?
Confectioner	Would you like anything else?
Alka	Yes, I'd like a quarter of a kilo of these chickpea-flour balls and five *rasgullas*, these cottage cheese balls, as well. Could you pack the *rasgullas* carefully so that none of the syrup leaks out.
Confectioner	Yes, of course, we'll pack them properly in a clay bowl.
Alka	Don't you sell *samosas* here?
Confectioner	Yes, we do, but they aren't ready yet. We start making *samosas* at four in the evening. Would you like some other savouries?
Alka	No, thank you, this is enough for today. Please make up my bill.

4.4   मसाले व खाने की सामग्री

 16

रसोई में

अलका	पल्लवी, मैं बहुत दिनों से तुमसे छोले बनाना सीखना चाहती थी।
पल्लवी	चलो, काम शुरू करते हैं। मैं काबुली चने उबालती हूँ। तब तक तुम यह दो प्याज़ छील कर महीन काटो।
अलका	छोले तुमने भिगोए थे? उन्हें पकने में कितनी देर लगेगी?
पल्लवी	इन्हें रात भर के लिए भिगोना और लगभग पचास मिनट या मुलायम होने तक उबालना होता है।
अलका	प्याज़ कट गए। इनका क्या करूँ?
पल्लवी	इस पतीले में मैं पाँच बड़े चम्मच तेल डाल रही हूँ। जब यह गरम हो जाए तो इस में एक तेजपत्ता, दो लौंग और दो इलायची डालना। उसके बाद प्याज़ डाल कर उन्हें धीमी आँच पर गुलाबी होने तक भूनना।
अलका	तुम लहसुन और अदरक पीस रही हो?
पल्लवी	हाँ। प्याज़ लाल हो गए? तो उन में यह लहसुन अदरक का लेप अच्छी तरह से मिलाकर भूनो। और अब मैं इसमें कुछ पिसे मसाले डालती हूँ।
अलका	कौन–से मसाले?
पल्लवी	एक–एक चम्मच हल्दी, ज़ीरा, धनिया, अमचूर, काली मिर्च और नमक। और थोड़ा–सा गरम मसाला भी। वैसे तो तुम बना–बनाया चना मसाला ख़रीद भी सकती हो।
अलका	इस मिश्रण में अभी और कुछ भी पड़ेगा?
पल्लवी	हाँ, मैं इसमें यह बारीक कटे हुए टमाटर डालती हूँ। इस पूरी सामग्री को आठ–दस मिनट के लिए मध्यम आँच पर तेल बाहर आने तक भूनना है। चलाती रहना, जिसमें मसाला लगे न।
अलका	वाह, कितनी बढ़िया महक है!
पल्लवी	अब इस में संभाल कर उबले हुए चने पानी के साथ मिलाते हैं। इन्हें दस मिनट तक खदबद करने देंगे, फिर हमारे छोले तैयार हैं। परसने से पहले तुम हरी धनिया महीन काट कर ऊपर से सजा सकती हो।

4.4 Spices and ingredients

In the kitchen

Alka	Pallavi, I've wanted to learn to cook chickpea curry from you for ages.
Pallavi	Come on, let's get down to work. I'll boil these chickpeas. You can peel the onions and chop them finely until then.
Alka	Had you soaked the chickpeas? How long will they need to be done?
Pallavi	They have to be soaked overnight and boiled for about fifty minutes or until they are soft.
Alka	The onions are chopped. What should I do with them?
Pallavi	I'm putting five teaspoons oil in this pan. When it becomes hot, put in a bay leaf, two cloves and two cardamoms. Then add the onions and fry them on low heat until they turn pinkish in colour.
Alka	Are you grinding the garlic and ginger?
Pallavi	Yes. Have the onions turned red? Then add this garlic and ginger paste to them, mix it in thoroughly and fry it. And now I'll put some ground spices into this.
Alka	Which ground spices?
Pallavi	A spoonful each of turmeric, cumin seeds, coriander, dried mango, pepper and salt. And a little *garam masala* as well. You can also buy a ready-made chickpea curry spice mix, though.
Alka	Does anything else go into this mixture?
Pallavi	Yes, I'll add these finely chopped tomatoes to it. The whole mixture has to be fried for 8 to 10 minutes on medium heat until the oil starts to leave it. Keep stirring so that the spices don't get burnt.
Alka	Wow, what a wonderful smell!
Pallavi	Now we'll carefully add the boiled chickpeas and water and let them simmer for ten minutes, then our chickpea curry is ready. Before serving it, you can chop some green coriander leaves finely and garnish it with them.

शब्दावली Glossary

४.१ 'मल्लिका' होटल में खाना: खाना मंगवाना
4.1 Eating at 'Mallika' restaurant: ordering a meal

खाना *m* 1. food 2. to eat *(verb)*
मंगवाना to order, to send for
मेनू *m* menu
पसंद करना to like, to choose
प्रकार *m* a kind, a sort, a type
पकवान *m* a delicacy, a dish
चुनना to choose, to select
आसान easy, simple
चीज़ *f* a thing
ख़याल *m* an opinion
तरह–तरह का many kinds of, various
व्यंजन *m* a dish
चखना to taste
आर्डर *m* an order (for food or drink)
गोश्त *m* meat, *also* mutton
के सिवा except, apart from
की तरह like, as
शाकाहारी a vegetarian
पनीर *m* a firm fresh cheese
पालक *m* spinach
सब्ज़ी *f* a vegetable; a vegetable dish
मसाला *m* spices, a spice
भिंडी *f* okra (a green vegetable)
आलू *m* a potato
गोभी *f* a cauliflower
शिमला–मिर्च *f* a pepper/a capsicum
भरवाँ *food* stuffed
मज़ेदार 1. interesting 2. *food* tasty
रसेदार, शोरबेदार cooked in a sauce or
            gravy
दाल *f* lentils, cooked lentils
दाल मक्खनी *f* black lentils cooked in a
            rich spicy sauce

मनपसंद liked, favourite
रायता *m* a side dish of finely chopped
            vegetables/fruits in yoghurt
ख़ीरा *m* a cucumber
तरकारी *f* green vegetables
बेचारा *m* a wretch, a helpless person
माँस–मछली *f* meat and fish
मतलब *m* a purpose/a meaning, sense
तंदूर *m* a traditional clay oven
पाक *m* a dish, something cooked
मुर्ग़ *m* chicken
मुर्ग़–टिक्का *m* skewered chunks of
            chicken grilled in a clay oven
अदरक *m* ginger
दही *m* yoghurt
काफ़ी enough
बैरा *m* a waiter
बुलाना to call, to summon, to send for
रुकना to stop
रोटी *f* a round unleavened flatbread
चावल *m* rice
भूलना to forget
सादा plain
पुलाव *m* pilau/pilaf: a spiced rice dish
            with vegetables or meat
नान *f* a leavened flatbread baked in a
            clay oven
बेशक undoubtedly, certainly
आख़िरी last, final
पन्ना *m* a page
टोकरी *f* a basket
पराठा/पराँठा *m* a fried flaky multi-
            layered flatbread
पूरा whole, complete

4.2 होटल में: खाने के पैसे चुकाना
4.2 In a restaurant: paying for the meal

चुकाना to settle, to pay
स्वादिष्ट tasty, delicious
ज़ायका *m* taste, flavour
मिर्च *f* a chilli; chilli powder
बिलकुल नहीं not at all
लज़ीज़ delicious, delightful
मीठा sweet
ख़ीर *f* a rice pudding
श्रीखंड *m* a creamy yoghurt pudding
कुलफ़ी *f* Indian ice cream
पिसता *m* a pistachio nut
ख़ासियत *f* a speciality
पेट *m* the stomach
भरना to be full
  पेट भरना to be sated/satiated/stuffed
बस enough
फटना to burst
ज़ायकेदार tasty, delicious

बिल *m* a bill
क्रेडिट-कार्ड *m* a credit card
अकेले alone, on one's own
थोड़े ही hardly, by no means
बाँटना to share
रिवाज *m* a custom, a practice
प्रथा *f* a tradition, a custom
प्रथानुसार according to custom
परंपरा *f* tradition
खिलाना to cause/invite to eat, to feed
ज़िम्मा *m* responsibility
उम्र *f* age
बड़ा senior in years, elder
सहमत होना to agree
अंधा-धुंध thoughtless, headlong
पालन *m* observing, complying
पालन करना to observe, to adhere to, to comply with

4.3 मिठाइयाँ: मिठाई की दुकान में
4.3 Indian sweets: in a sweet shop

मिठाई *f* a sweet
दुकान *m* a shop
पीला yellow
बरफ़ी / बर्फ़ी *f* a rectangular sweet made from sugar and thickened milk or nuts
बनना to be made/prepared
हलवाई *m* sweet-maker, sweet-seller, confectioner
ख़ोया / ख़ोआ *m* thickened milk
केसर *m* saffron
पड़ना to be found, to be put

कलाकंद *m* a sweet made of cream cheese, milk and sugar
मिला-जुला mixed, assorted
चलना to last, to not spoil/decay
ख़राब bad, spoiled
मेवा *m* dried fruits, nuts
आराम से unhurriedly, gently
बादाम *m* an almond
ताज़ा fresh
चखना to taste
वास्तव *m* में in reality, actually
हिसाब *m* a fixed price, rate

किलो *m* a kilogramme
डिब्बा *m* a box, carton
अंजीर *f* a fig
काजू *m* a cashew nut
कतली *f* a type of sweet cut into thin
            slices
उपहार *m* a gift
पैक करना to pack
पाव *m* a quarter
बेसन *m* gram/chickpea flour
लड्डू *m* a sweet ball made of flour,
            thickened milk, etc. mixed
            with sugar, nuts, raisins, etc.
रसगुल्ला *m* a sweet spongy ball of
            soft cheese soaked in syrup

संभाल कर with care, carefully
शीरा *f* a sugar syrup
चूना to drip, to leak
कुल्हड़ *m* an earthenware cup
बांधना to pack
समोसा *m* a fried triangular-shaped
            pasty with a savoury filling
तैयार ready
शाम *f* the evening
चार बजे four o'clock
शुरू करना to begin
नमकीन *m* a savoury snack, savouries
काफ़ी 1. enough
हिसाब *m* 1. a fixed price 2. accounts
हिसाब करना to calculate an account

४.४ मसाले व खाने की सामग्री: रसोई में
4.4 Spices and ingredients: in the kitchen

मसाला *m* spices, a spice
सामग्री *f* materials, ingredients
रसोई *f* a kitchen
छोले *pl* chickpeas
बनाना to make, to prepare (food, etc.)
सीखना to learn
काबुली चना *m* a chickpea
उबालना to boil
प्याज़ *m* an onion
छीलना to skin, to peel, to pare
महीन 1. fine 2. thin
काटना to cut
भिगोना to wet, to soak, to steep
पकना to be cooked
रात भर the whole night
लगभग approximately
मुलायम soft

पतीला *m* a wide mouthed pot or pan
चम्मच *m* a spoon
तेल *m* oil
डालना to put in, to add
गरम hot, warm
तेजपत्ता *m* a bay-leaf
लौंग *m* a clove
इलायची *f* cardamom
धीमा low
आँच *f* a flame, heat
गुलाबी pink
भूनना to roast, to fry
लहसुन *m* garlic
लेप *m* a paste
अच्छी तरह से well, thoroughly
हल्दी *f* turmeric
जीरा *m* cumin

धनिया *f/m* coriander
अमचूर *m* dried mango powder
काली मिर्च *f* black pepper
नमक *m* salt
गरम मसाला *m* an aromatic mixture of
                    ground spices which
                    gives a hot taste to food
वैसे तो on the whole, in fact
बना–बनाया ready-made
ख़रीदना to buy
मिश्रण *m* a mixture
बारीक fine, thin
टमाटर *m* a tomato
पूरा whole, complete

मध्यम medium, moderate
आँच *f* flame, heat
बाहर आना to come out
चलाना to stir
लगना *cooking* to be burnt
महक *f* fragrance, an aroma
उबला हुआ boiled
पानी *m* water
खदबद करना to boil, to simmer
परसना / परोसना to serve food
हरा green
हरी धनिया *f* fresh coriander leaves
सजाना to arrange, to prepare,
                    to decorate

5
ख़रीदारी
Shopping

5.1 वस्त्रों की दुकान में

कपड़े ख़रीदना

अजय	यह रंग-बिरंगे कुरते औरतों के लिए हैं या आदमियों के लिए?
बेचनेवाली	यह सब कपड़े पुरुषों के लिए ही हैं। महिलाओं के वस्त्र उस तरफ़ हैं। आपको कौन-सा रंग दिखाऊँ?
अजय	मुझे रंगीन नहीं बल्कि एकदम सीधा-सादा सफ़ेद रंग का कुरता-पाजामा चाहिए।
बेचनेवाली	आप को अपने लिए चाहिए? यह लीजिए सफ़ेद कुरता और यह है आपकी नाप का पाजामा।
अजय	क्या दाम है इनका?

बेचनेवाली	दाम परची पर लिखा होगा ... कुरता एक सौ पचहत्तर रुपए का और पाजामा एक सौ तीस का। आजकल हमारे बने-बनाए कपड़ों पर दस प्रतिशत की छूट है इसलिए दोनों मिला कर दो सौ पचहत्तर रूपए हुए।
अजय	बहुत अच्छा, इन दोनों को हमारे लिए अलग रख दीजिए।
आन्या	इस कुरते का कपड़ा कितना महीन है! क्या यह रेशम है?
बेचनेवाली	जी नहीं, यह सूती कपड़ा ही है। गरमी में पहनने में यह बहुत आरामदेह होता है।
आन्या	ऐसे ही कपड़े की कुरती या कमीज़ मेरे लिए भी मिलेगी?
बेचनेवाली	क्यों नहीं। उधर सब वस्त्र महिलाओं के लिए हैं: इस गड्डी में लंबे कुरते हैं, छपे हुए और कढ़ाई के साथ भी। इधर कुरतियाँ और शलवार कमीज़ के जोड़े हैं।
आन्या	मुझे उस गड्डी में वह नीली कुरती दिखाइए और उसके नीचे जो हलके गुलाबी रंग की कमीज़ है, वह भी। क्या यह मेरी नाप में मिलेगी?
बेचनेवाली	यह आप को पूरा आना चाहिए, लेकिन बायीं ओर पर ट्राइ-रूम है, आप पहन कर देख सकती हैं।
आन्या	(कमीज़ पहन कर) यह मुझ पर कैसी लगती है?
बेचनेवाली	आपके ऊपर गुलाबी रंग बहुत जँच रहा है, मैडम।
अजय	रंग तो सुन्दर है, आन्या, लेकिन कमीज़ तुम्हारे लिए ज़रा बड़ी नहीं है?
आन्या	हाँ, कुछ ठीक नहीं बैठती। यह वाली ज़्यादा ढीली है और इससे छोटी नाप की बहुत तंग थी।
अजय	तो फिर तुम कपड़ा खरीद लो और कमीज़ दर्ज़ी से सिलवा लेना।
बेचनेवाली	अगर आप चाहें तो यही कपड़ा थान में से कटवा सकती हैं। आप की कमीज़ में करीब दो मीटर कपड़ा लगेगा।

5.1   In a clothes shop

Buying clothes

Ajay	Are these multicoloured shirts for women or for men?
Saleswoman	All these garments are for men. Women's clothes are on the other side. What colour can I show you?
Ajay	I want an absolutely plain white *kurta-pyjama* suit, nothing coloured.
Saleswoman	Do you want it for yourself? Here you are - a white *kurta*, and here's a pair of loose trousers in your size.

Ajay	How much do they cost?
Saleswoman	The price should be on the label... the *kurta* is 175 rupees and the trousers 130. There's a ten percent discount on our readymade garments these days, so that makes 275 rupees for the two of them.
Ajay	Oh good! Please keep these two aside for me.
Anja	What fine material this shirt is made of! Is this silk?
Saleswoman	No, it's cotton. It's very comfortable to wear in summer.
Anja	Would I find a shirt of this material for myself, too?
Saleswoman	Certainly. All the clothes on that side are for women: there are long tunics in this pile, printed and embroidered ones as well. Shorter tunics and *salwar-kameez* suits are over here.
Anja	Could you show me the blue tunic in that pile and the light pink one below it as well? Do you have these in my size?
Saleswoman	This should fit you. But there is a fitting room on the left, you can try them on and see.
Anja	(having put on the tunic) How does this look on me?
Saleswoman	The pink is very becoming, Madam.
Ajay	The colour is pretty, Anja, but isn't the tunic a little too large for you?
Anja	Yes, it doesn't fit too well. This one is too loose and the one a size smaller was too tight.
Ajay	Then just buy the fabric and have your tunics tailored.
Saleswoman	You can have the same material cut from the roll, if you like. You'll need about two metres of fabric for a tunic.

5.2   मोल–भाव करना

फलवाले से आम ख़रीदना

पल्लवी	ये आम कितने के हैं?
फलवाला	लीजिए, आम लीजिए, बहनजी। बहुत बढ़िया हैं यह। कितने लेंगी? दो दर्जन? तीन दर्जन?
पल्लवी	लेकिन पहले इनका दाम तो बताइए।
फलवाला	सिर्फ़ ढाई सौ रुपये दर्जन।

पल्लवी	क्या? इतना महँगा? मगर सामने वाली दुकान में तो आम पचास रुपये किलो हैं।
फलवाला	अरे मैडम जी, क्या कह रही हैं आप! वे होंगे और किसी तरह के आम। ये तो रतनागिरी के हाफ़ुस हैं, महाराष्ट्र के ख़ास आम और सारी दुनिया में मशहूर।
पल्लवी	अच्छा? तो ये आल्फ़ोंज़ो आम हैं? मीठे भी होते हैं?
फलवाला	मीठे? अरे, शहद से भी ज़्यादा! आप आज ही ढेर-से ले जाइए, क्या पता कि कल मिलें या न मिलें। वैसे भी ये ज़्यादातर भारत के बाहर जाते है।
पल्लवी	अच्छा, आप के कहने पर मैं लेकर देखती हूँ, लेकिन इस दाम पर नहीं। ढाई सौ रुपए, बाप रे बाप!
फलवाला	चलिए, आप के लिए कम कर देता हूँ। दो रुपए कम दीजिएगा।
पल्लवी	दो रुपए से क्या फ़र्क पड़ेगा? मैं दर्जन के दो सौ तीस रुपए दूँगी, उससे ऊपर एक पैसा भी नहीं।
फलवाला	दो सौ तीस! इस दाम पर तो मैं ख़ुद ख़रीदता हूँ। अच्छा ठीक है, दो सौ चालीस कर देता हूँ, लेकिन सिर्फ़ आप के लिए। कितने आम दूँ? तीन दर्जन?
पल्लवी	नहीं, नहीं, इतने आम कौन खाएगा! एक दर्जन, बस।
फलवाला	और क्या लेंगी? सेब, अंगूर, केले? संतरे ले जाइए, ये आज ही नागपुर से आए है, एकदम ताज़े और रसभरे।
पल्लवी	नहीं, आज के लिए ये आम ही बहुत है। यह लीजिए आप के पैसे।

5.2   Haggling

Buying mangoes from a fruit vendor

Pallavi	How much are these mangoes?
Fruit vendor	Yes, here you are, ma'am, buy these mangoes. They are very good indeed. How many would you like? Two dozen? Three dozen?
Pallavi	But tell me the price first.
Fruit vendor	Only two hundred fifty rupees a dozen.
Pallavi	What? So much? But in the shop across the road mangoes are 50 rupees a kilo.
Fruit vendor	Oh come, Madam-ji, what are you saying? They must be mangoes of a different sort. These ones are Alphonsos

	from Ratnagiri, very special mangoes from Maharashtra and famous throughout the world.
Pallavi	Really? So these are Alphosos? Are they at all sweet?
Fruit vendor	Sweet? Even sweeter than honey! You'd better buy a whole lot today, who knows if you'll get any tomorrow. As it is, most of them are sent out of India.
Pallavi	Well, all right, since you insist, I'll try them, but not at this price. 250 rupees, good grief!
Fruit vendor	Oh, well, seeing it's you, I'll reduce the price. Give me two rupees less.
Pallavi	What difference is two rupees going to make? I'll pay 230 rupees a dozen, not a paisa more.
Fruit vendor	Two hundred thirty! That's the price I buy them at myself. All right then, I'll make it two forty, but only for you. How many mangoes should I give you? Three dozen?
Pallavi	No, no, who's going to eat so many? A dozen, that's all.
Fruit vendor	And what else? Apples, grapes, bananas? Won't you take some oranges too, they've only come in from Nagpur today, really fresh and juicy.
Pallavi	No, thanks, the mangoes are quite enough for today. Here's your money.

5.3   किताब–घर में

हिन्दी की किताबें मँगवाना

अजय	आप मेरी सहायता कर सकते हैं?
विक्रेता	जी हाँ, कहिए?
अजय	मैं भीष्म साहनी का उपन्यास 'तमस्' ढूँढ रहा हूँ, लेकिन आपकी दुकान में कहीं दिखाई नहीं दे रहा है।
विक्रेता	'तमस्'? यह तो हमारे पास होना चाहिए। मैं देखता हूँ ... यह लीजिए आप का उपन्यास।
अजय	लेकिन यह तो उसका अंग्रेज़ी अनुवाद है। मुझे मूल–भाषा में चाहिए, यानी हिन्दी में।
विक्रेता	अच्छा, तब तो हिन्दी विभाग में देखना पड़ेगा। मेरे साथ चलिए, हमारा हिन्दी विभाग ऊपर है।

अजय	मुझे एक अच्छे हिन्दी शब्द-कोश की भी ख़ोज है।
विक्रेता	हमारे अनेक शब्द-कोश यहाँ हैं: हिन्दी, हिन्दी-अंगेज़ी, उर्दू-हिन्दी वग़ैरह। लेकिन 'तमस्' उपन्यास अभी दुकान में नहीं है। यदि आप चाहें तो आप के लिए मँगा सकता हूँ।
अजय	मँगवाने पर पुस्तक कब तक मिल जाती है?
विक्रेता	दो-तीन दिन लगते हैं, उससे अधिक नहीं।
अजय	ठीक है, मेरी सूची पर अन्य पुस्तकें भी हैं जो मुझे आप के पास नहीं मिलीं। उन्हें भी मँगा दीजिएगा।
विक्रेता	अवश्य। अपना नाम और टेलीफ़ोन नंबर मेरे पास छोड़ जाइएगा। किताबें जैसे ही आएँगी, हम आप को सूचित कर देंगे।
अजय	धन्यवाद।

5.3   In a bookshop

Ordering Hindi books

Ajay	I wonder if you could help me.
Bookseller	Yes, what can I do for you?
Ajay	I'm looking for Bhisham Sahni's novel 'Tamas', but I can't see it anywhere in your shop.
Bookseller	'Tamas'? We should have it. I'll take a look … here you are – there's your novel.
Ajay	But this is the English translation. I need the original, in Hindi, that is.
Bookseller	Right; then we'll have to look in the Hindi department. The Hindi department is upstairs, if you'll come with me.
Ajay	I'm also looking for a good Hindi dictionary.
Bookseller	We have several dictionaries. Here: Hindi, Hindi-English, Urdu-Hindi, and so on. But the novel 'Tamas' is not in stock at present. I can order it for you if you like.
Ajay	How long will it take if I order it?
Bookseller	It takes two to three days, not more than that.
Ajay	Right. There are other books on my list, too, that I didn't find in your shop. Please order them as well.
Bookseller	Certainly. Just leave your name and telephone number with me. We'll inform you as soon as the books arrive.
Ajay	Thank you.

शब्दावली   Glossary

5.1 वस्त्रों की दुकान में: कपड़े ख़रीदना
5.1 In a clothes shop: buying clothes

वस्त्र *m* clothes
दुकान *f* a shop
कपड़ा *m* 1. clothes, garment 2. cloth
रंग *m* a colour
रंग–बिरंगा multicoloured
कुरता / कुर्ता *m* a loose, collarless shirt
औरत *f* a woman
आदमी *m* a man, a person
बेचनेवाली *f* a saleswoman
पुरुष *m* a man
महिला *f* a woman
कौन–सा which
रंगीन coloured, colourful
बल्कि but rather
एकदम completely
सीधा–सादा plain, unadorned, simple
सफ़ेद *m* white
पाजामा *m* loose cotton trousers
नाप *f* size, measure
दाम *m* a price, cost
परची *f* / परचा *m* a label, a piece of
                            paper
आजकल nowadays, recently
बना–बनाया ready-made
प्रतिशत *f* per cent
दोनों the two, both
अलग separately
रखना to keep, to put aside
महीन 1. fine 2. thin
रेशम *m* silk

सूती made of cotton
गरमी / गर्मी *f* 1. heat 2. summer
पहनना to put on (clothes), to wear
आरामदेह comfortable
कुरती *f* a blouse, a short tunic
कमीज़ *f* a shirt/a tunic
गड्डी *f* a heap, a pile
लंबा long
छपना to be printed
कढ़ाई *f* embroidery
शलवार *m* loose pleated trousers with
                            a drawstring waist
 शलवार–कमीज़ *f* a suit consisting of
                            loose trousers com-
                            bined with a tunic
जोड़ा *m* a pair
नीला blue
हलका light, pale (*colour*)
गुलाबी pink
पूरा आना to fit
ट्राइ–रूम *m* a fitting/dressing room
जँचना to seem good, to suit
ज़रा a little
बड़ा big, large
ढीला loose
तंग tight
दर्ज़ी *m* a tailor
सिलवाना to have something sewn
थान *m* a piece, a bolt (of cloth)
कटवाना to cause to be cut
मीटर *m* a metre

5.2 मोल–भाव करना: फलवाले से आम ख़रीदना
5.2 Haggling: buying mangoes from a fruit vendor

मोल–भाव *m*   bargaining, haggling

फल *m*   fruit

फलवाला *f*   a fruit seller/vendor

आम *m*   a mango

दर्जन *m*   a dozen

ढाई   two and a half

मगर   but

किलो *m*   a kilo

रतनागिरी *m*   Ratnagiri (a town in the state of Maharashtra)

हाफ़ुस, आल्फ़ौंज़ो *m*   a variety of mango

महाराष्ट्र *m*   Maharashtra (Indian state)

ख़ास   choice, best

सारा   all, whole, entire

दुनिया *f*   the world

मशहूर   famous

मीठा   sweet

शहद *m*   honey

ज़्यादा   more

ढेर–से   a great number, many

पता होना *m*   to know

कल *m*   tomorrow

मिलना   to be found; available

ज़्यादातर   most, most commonly

बाहर *m*   outside

कहना *m*   advice

बाप रे बाप!   *interjection* good heavens! *expressing surprise or grief*

कम   1. little, few 2. less

कम करना   to reduce, to decrease

फ़र्क *m*   difference

ऊपर   over, above

पैसा *m*   1. money 2. a coin equal in value to 1/100th of a rupee

ख़ुद   self (myself, himself, itself, etc.)

सेब *m*   an apple

अंगूर *m*   a grape

केला *m*   a banana

नागपुर   Nagpur (a city in the state of Maharashtra)

ताज़ा   fresh

रसभरा   juicy

बहुत   1. enough 2. ample

5.3 किताब–घर में: हिन्दी की पुस्तकों मँगवाना
5.3 In a bookshop: ordering Hindi books

किताब *f*   a book

किताब–घर *m*   a bookshop

सहायता *f*   help, assistance, aid

विक्रेता *m*   a salesman, a trader

उपन्यास *m*   a novel

ढूँढना   to look for, to search out

अनुवाद *m*   a translation

मूल   original

भाषा *f*   a language

विभाग *m*   a department

शब्द–कोश *m*   a dictionary

खोज *f*   search

वग़ैरह   and so forth, et cetera

अधिक   more

सूची *f*   a list

अन्य   other, different

पुस्तक *f*   a book

अवश्य   certainly, of course

टेलीफ़ोन नंबर *m*   a telephone number

छोड़ना   to leave

जैसे ही   as soon as

सूचित करना   to inform

6

स्वास्थ्य-संबंधी
Health matters

6.1 बाज़ार में आपात-स्थिति

20

बेहोश हो जाना

दुकानवाला	अरे, अरे, इन महिला को कोई संभालो! ये शायद बेहोश हो गई हैं।
राह–चलते	क्या हुआ? ये बहनजी चलते-चलते अचानक गिर गई। लगता है बेहोश हो गई हैं। इनको पंखा करो! इनके मुँह पर पानी के छींटे डालो! पानी लाओ, जल्दी पानी लाओ!
पल्लवी	आप लोग शांत रहिए और ज़रा मुझे रास्ता दीजिए, ये मेरे साथ हैं। क्या हुआ इन्हें?

दुकानवाला	ये अभी–अभी मेरी दुकान से सामान लेकर निकलीं और अचानक सड़क पर बेहोश हो कर गिर गईं। देखिए, शायद इन्हें होश आ रहा है।
अलका	उफ़ … यह क्या हो रहा है … क्या हुआ?
पल्लवी	आराम से, आराम से! जल्दी में मत उठो। बिलकुल धीरे-धीरे। तुम बेहोश होकर गिर गई थीं, लेकिन घबराने की कोई बात नहीं है।
दुकानवाला	इनको इस कुर्सी पर बैठा दीजिए।
राह–चलता	इधर धूप बहुत तेज़ है — कुर्सी को पेड़ के नीचे छाँह में रखो।
पल्लवी	धन्यवाद। वहाँ तक चल पाओगी, अलका? (दुकानवाले से) इन के लिए एक पेप्सी कोला दीजिएगा।
अलका	हाँ, हाँ, अब मैं बिलकुल ठीक हूँ। पता नहीं क्यों मुझे एकाएक चक्कर आ गया था। क्या मैं बहुत देर तक बेहोश रही?
दुकानवाला	नहीं, सिर्फ़ कुछ पल। लेकिन आप धड़ाम से गिरीं, सो लोग डर गए।
पल्लवी	तुम्हें कहीं चोट तो नहीं आई है? यह क्या है, तुम्हारी कुहनी से ख़ून बह रहा है?
दुकानवाला	यह लीजिए, आपका पेप्सी। डॉक्टर की क्लिनिक पास में ही है और डाक्टर साहब आज इतवार के दिन भी बैठते हैं।
अलका	नहीं, यह तो बहुत मामूली चोट है, इसके लिए डाक्टर की क्या ज़रूरत। गिरते समय कुहनी शायद ज़रा छिल गई है, और कुछ नहीं है।
पल्लवी	फिर भी डाक्टर को दिखा लेना चाहिए। आख़िर बेहोशी का कुछ कारण रहा होगा।
अलका	कारण तो ज़ाहिर है — मैं काफ़ी देर से कड़ी धूप में धूम रही हूँ। ऊपर से आज पानी भी बहुत कम पिया है। वैसे भी मेरा रक्त दबाव कम रहता है। गर्मी और पानी की कमी की वजह से यह हुआ होगा।
दुकानवाला	हाँ, आप ठीक कहती हैं। आप घर पर आराम कीजिए और काफ़ी पानी पीजिएगा।
अलका	जी हाँ, शुक्रिया। चलो पल्लवी, अब घर चलते हैं।
पल्लवी	ऐसी हालत में तुम रिक्शे पर जाना चाहती हो! तुम धीरे-धीरे अपना पेप्सी पियो और पाँच-दस मिनट इंतज़ार करो। मैं राजन को फ़ोन करके कहती हूँ कि वह गाड़ी ले कर आए।
अलका	उन्हें तकलीफ़ क्यों देती हो, वह भी छुट्टी के दिन?

पल्लवी	तो क्या हुआ? अगर तुम डाक्टर के पास नहीं जाती हो तो डाक्टर को तुम्हारे पास आना पड़ेगा!

6.1   An emergency in the marketplace

Fainting

Shopkeeper	Hey, hey, someone help this lady here! She seems to have fainted.
Passersby	What happened? Suddenly, while walking, this lady fell down. She seems to have fainted. Fan her! Sprinkle some water on her face! Get some water, quickly get some water!
Pallavi	Could you all please calm down and let me through, she is with me. What happened to her?
Shopkeeper	She left my shop just now, having made some purchases, and suddenly collapsed on the road. Look, perhaps she's coming to…
Alka	Uh… What's happening… what happened?
Pallavi	Easy, easy does it! Don't get up in a hurry. Very slowly now. You fainted and fell, but there's no need to be alarmed.
Shopkeeper	Here, get her to sit on this chair.
Passerby	The sun is much too strong here – put the chair in the shade under the tree.
Pallavi	Thank you. Can you manage to walk that far, Alka? (To the shopkeeper) Would you give me a Pepsi for her, please?
Alka	Yes, yes, I'm perfectly all right now. I've no idea why I suddenly got dizzy. Was I unconscious for long?
Shopkeeper	No, just for a few seconds. But you fell with a great thud, so people got scared.
Pallavi	You haven't hurt yourself anywhere, have you? What's this, is your elbow bleeding?
Shopkeeper	Here's your Pepsi. There's a doctor's clinic nearby and the doctor is in on Sundays, too.
Alka	No, no, this is just a slight injury, there's no need for a doctor. I must have grazed my elbow when I fell, it's no more than that.

Pallavi	Even so, you should see a doctor. After all there must be a reason why you fainted.
Alka	The reason is obvious – I've been wandering around in the harsh sunshine for quite a while. Besides, I've had very little water to drink today. Even otherwise, my blood pressure tends to be low. This must have happened because of the heat and the lack of water.
Shopkeeper	Yes, you're right. You should rest at home and drink plenty of fluids.
Alka	Yes, thank you. Come on, Pallavi, let's head home now.
Pallavi	You're thinking of taking a rickshaw in this condition! Just drink your Pepsi slowly and wait for five or ten minutes. I'll ring Rajan up and tell him to come here in the car.
Alka	Why do want to bother him, that too on a holiday?
Pallavi	So what? If you won't go to the doctor, the doctor will have to come to you!

6.2 घर में आपात-स्थिति

21

पेट की गड़बड़ी

पल्लवी	नमस्ते, अजय जी। इतनी जल्दी में कहाँ जा रहे हैं?
अजय	नमस्ते, मैं आप ही के पास आ रहा था। आप लोग शायद कहीं बाहर गए थे।
राजन	हाँ, पल्लवी की सहेली की तबीयत ठीक नहीं थी इसलिए उसे घर छोड़ने गए थे।
पल्लवी	क्या बात है, आप बहुत परेशान नज़र आ रहे हैं।
अजय	जी हाँ, बड़ी मुसीबत में हूँ। आन्या बीमार पड़ गई है और हमारे डाक्टर रविवार को मिलते नहीं। कल रात से उसकी हालत बहुत ख़राब है।
राजन	अरे! क्या हो गया उन्हें?
अजय	उसका बुरी तरह से पेट ख़राब है। बार-बार उसको उलटी और दस्त हो रहे हैं, और पेट में ऐंठन भी हो रही है। इस सब की वजह से उसे बहुत कमज़ोरी महसूस हो रही है। मैं समझ नहीं पा रहा हूँ कि उसे तुरंत

हस्पताल ले जाना चाहिए या नहीं। कहीं यह हैज़ा तो नहीं है? आप की
राय लेने आ रहा था।

पल्लवी   आप के फ़्लैट का दरवाज़ा खुला है? तो मैं आन्या के पास जाती हूँ।

राजन   हैज़ा? उस के लक्षण तो साफ़ होते हैं। पेट में दर्द या अन्य कोई
           तकलीफ़ नहीं होती। और उलटियों की संख्या बढ़ती जाती है।

अजय   नहीं, उलटियाँ तो काफ़ी कम हो गई हैं, बस उसे मतली आ रही है।

राजन   तब तो यह रोग कॉलेरा नहीं हो सकता, क्योंकि उस में जी नहीं
           मचलाता। मालूम होता है कि आन्या ने कोई ग़लत खाना खा लिया है।

अजय   जी हाँ, उस ने रात के खाने के बाद आइस-क्रीम खाई थी जो तीन-चार
           दिन से फ़्रिज में रखी हुई थी और शायद ख़राब हो गई थी। उसे खाने
           के कुछ ही देर बाद उसका पेट गड़बड़ हो गया।

राजन   तब तो स्पष्ट है कि उसे आहार विषाक्तन हो गया है। शरीर संदूषित
           पदार्थ को निकालने की कोशिश कर रहा है। उसे रोकना नहीं
           चाहिए। दो दिन में पेट ख़ुद ही ठीक हो जाता है।

अजय   तो ख़तरे की कोई बात नहीं है?

राजन   ख़तरा सिर्फ़ यह होता है कि शरीर में पानी और लवण की कमी हो
           सकती है। इन की पूर्ति करने के लिए आप आन्या को लवण घोल कर
           पानी पिलाते रहिए।

पल्लवी   बेचारी आन्या बिलकुल थक गई है, लेकिन उस की हालत में धीरे-धीरे
           सुधार हो रहा है। अजय जी, आप के पास इलेक्ट्रोलाइट न हो तो मैं
           दवा-ख़ाने से ले आती हूँ।

अजय   अरे नहीं, आप कष्ट क्यों उठाती हैं, मैं ख़ुद ही ले आऊँगा।

पल्लवी   इस में कष्ट कैसा? दो कदम की दूरी पर ही तो है। वैसे भी मुझे वहाँ
           जाना था, कुछ दवाएँ ख़रीदनी हैं। आप आन्या के पास रहिए।

अजय   आप लोगों की बहुत मेहरबानी है।

6.2   An emergency at home

A stomach upset

Pallavi   Hello, Ajay-ji. Where are you off to in such a hurry?
Ajay   Hello, it was you I was coming to see. It seems you'd gone
             out somewhere.
Rajan   Yes, Pallavi's friend wasn't well, so we'd gone to drop her
             home.

Pallavi	What's the matter? You look very worried.
Ajay	Yes, I'm in great difficulty. Anja has fallen ill and our doctor is not available on Sunday. She's been in very bad shape since last night.
Rajan	Oh, dear! What's wrong with her?
Ajay	Her stomach is badly upset. She has been throwing up again and again and has diarrhoea and abdominal cramps as well. Because of all this she's feeling very weak. I can't decide if she should be taken to the hospital immediately or not. What if it's cholera? I was coming to ask for your advice.
Pallavi	Is the door to your flat open? Then I'll go to Anja.
Rajan	Cholera? That has very distinct symptoms. There's no stomach ache, nor any other complaints. And the vomiting keeps increasing.
Ajay	No, the vomiting has decreased quite a bit now, only she's feeling nauseous.
Rajan	Then it can't be cholera, because it doesn't cause nausea. It looks like Anja has eaten something that didn't agree with her.
Ajay	Yes, after dinner she ate some ice cream that had been lying in the fridge for three or four days and might have spoiled. Her stomach got upset shortly after eating it.
Rajan	Then it's clearly a case of food-poisoning. Her body is trying to get rid of the contaminated substance. It shouldn't be stopped. The stomach returns to normal by itself in two days' time.
Ajay	It's nothing dangerous, then?
Rajan	The only risk is the body can lose too much fluid and salts. To replace these, keep giving Anja water with oral rehydration salts dissolved in it.
Pallavi	Poor Anja is completely exhausted, but her condition is gradually improving. Ajay-ji, if you don't have any electrolyte solution, I'll get it from the chemist.
Ajay	Oh, no, please don't go to all that trouble, I'll get it myself.
Pallavi	It's no trouble at all. It's just a stone's throw from here. I had to go there anyway, I need to buy some medicines. You stay here with Anja.
Ajay	It is really most kind of you both.

6.3 औषधालय/दवा-ख़ाने में

दवाएँ ख़रीदना

औषधिविक्रेता	नमस्ते, मैडम जी। आपकी क्या सेवा कर सकता हूँ?
पल्लवी	सब से पहले मुझे इलेट्राल दीजिए।
विक्रेता	पाँच सौ ग्राम का पैकेट चाहिए या ये छोटे पाउच?
पल्लवी	इतनी छोटी थैलियाँ? इन का क्या फ़ायदा है?
विक्रेता	पाउडर को नापना नहीं पड़ता है — एक थैली भर इलेक्ट्राल एक लिटर पानी के लिए है।
पल्लवी	अच्छा, मुझे पंद्रह छोटी थैलियाँ दे दीजिए। और मुझे सिर-दर्द की गोली का एक पत्ता भी दीजिए।
विक्रेता	कौन-सी गोली? क्रोसिन?
पल्लवी	हाँ, क्रोसिन ठीक रहेगी। इन दोनों दवाओं के अलावा मुझे कोई असरदार मच्छर भगाने वाला लोशन या लेप भी चाहिए।
विक्रेता	हाल में कुछ नए पदार्थ निकले हैं। एक यह है: गुड नाइट, और यह है ओडोमॉस।
पल्लवी	ओडोमॉस! यह तो निहायत बदबूदार और चिपचिपी चीज़ होती है। इसे आप ही रखिए।
विक्रेता	नहीं मैडम, यह नया ओडोमॉस पहले से बहुत सुधरा हुआ है। आप ने टीवी में इस का विज्ञापन नहीं देखा? यह अब लेप नहीं, बल्कि क्रीम है, सुगंधित भी है और बिलकुल चिप-चिप नहीं करती।
पल्लवी	अच्छा? आप ने ख़ुद कभी इस का इस्तेमाल किया है?
विक्रेता	हाँ, क्यों नहीं, अक्सर किया है। मेरी बीवी तो यह क्रीम हमारी साल-भर की बच्ची के चेहरे पर भी लगाती है क्योंकि इस से छोटे बच्चों की त्वचा को नुकसान नहीं पहुँचता।
पल्लवी	उम्मीद है कि मच्छरों को नुकसान पहुँचता होगा! ठीक है, इसका एक ट्यूब परखने के लिए मैं भी ले जाती हूँ। बस, हो गया। मेरा बिल बना दीजिए।

6.3   At the chemist's

Buying medicine

Chemist	Good afternoon, madam. What can I do for you?
Pallavi	First of all, please give me some Electral.
Chemist	Would you like a 500 gram packet or these small sachets?
Pallavi	Such small sachets? What use are they?
Chemist	The powder doesn't have to be measured out – one sachet is meant for one litre of water.
Pallavi	Fine, then please give me 15 small packets. And a strip of headache tablets as well.
Chemist	Which tablets? Crocin?
Pallavi	Yes, Crocin is fine. Apart from these two medicines, I also need an effective mosquito repellent lotion or ointment.
Chemist	Some new products have come out recently. Here's one: Good Knight, and this is Odomos.
Pallavi	Odomos! That's an extremely smelly, sticky thing. You'd better keep it yourself.
Chemist	No, madam, this new Odomos is much better than before. Haven't you seen the ad on TV? It's not an ointment any longer, instead it's a cream, fragrant and not sticky at all.
Pallavi	Really? Have you ever used it yourself?
Chemist	Yes, of course, often. In fact, my wife applies it on our one-year-old baby's face too, because it doesn't cause any harm to baby skin.
Pallavi	Well, I hope it causes harm to the mosquitoes! All right then, I'll take a tube of it, too, to try out. That's it. Please make up my bill.

6.4   डाक्टर से परामर्श करना

खाँसी, गला ख़राब होना

पल्लवी	नमस्ते, डाक्टर साहब।
डा. भट	बैठिए, मिसिज़ जैन। आपको क्या तकलीफ़ है?

पल्लवी	कई दिन से मेरा गला ख़राब है। गले में दर्द है और ख़ाँस-ख़ाँस कर परेशान हूँ।
डा. भट	सूखी ख़ाँसी आती है या बलग़म के साथ?
पल्लवी	शुरू में मुझे सूखी ख़ाँसी आती थी लेकिन तीन दिन से ख़ाँसते समय पीला-सा बलग़म भी आता है।
डा. भट	ख़ाँसी शुरू हुए कितने दिन हो गए?
पल्लवी	दस दिन हो रहे हैं। पहले कम थी लेकिन दिन पर दिन बदतर होती जा रही है। अब साँस लेने में भी थोड़ी तकलीफ़ होने लगी है।
डा. भट	जुकाम के कोई लक्षण भी हैं? नाक बहती है, बुख़ार है?
पल्लवी	थे, लेकिन अब नहीं हैं। जुकाम ही के साथ ख़ाँसी शुरू हुई थी। दो दिन तेज़ बुख़ार भी था, फिर वह आप से आप ही उतर गया। अब जुकाम तो ठीक हो गया लेकिन ख़ाँसी से छुटकारा नहीं मिल रहा है।
डा. भट	अपनी कलाई आगे कीजिए, मैं आप की नाड़ी देखूँगा। अब मुँह ख़ोलिए, जीभ बाहर निकालिए, "आ" कहिए। गले में दर्द है? अब यहाँ लेट जाइए। लंबी साँस लीजिए ... हाँ, एक बार फिर ... साँस लेते समय यह सूँ-सूँ की आवाज़ कब से आ रही है? यहाँ दबाने से छाती में दर्द होता है?
पल्लवी	ऐसे नहीं, पर कभी-कभी जब बहुत ज़ोर से ख़ाँसी का दौरा आता है, तब।
डा. भट	अब आप उठ सकती हैं। मैं आपके लिए नुस़ख़ा लिख देता हूँ। आपको तीव्र ब्रांकाइटिस हो गया है।
पल्लवी	अरे बाप रे!
डा. भट	चिंता की कोई बात नहीं है, इस रोग के इलाज में आम तौर पर कोई कठिनाई नहीं होती। बस आपको पाँच दिन तक ऐंटीबायोटिक दवाएँ लेनी होंगी क्योंकि यह जीवाणु का यानि बैक्टीरियल संक्रमण बन चुका है।
पल्लवी	यह ख़ाँसी मुझे बहुत तंग करती है, डाक्टर। रात की नींद ख़राब कर देती है।
डा. भट	हाँ, जो नुस़ख़ा मैं लिख रहा हूँ उस में एक बलग़म निकालने की दवा भी है। इसके अलावा आप बलग़म पतला करने के लिए थोड़ी-थोड़ी देर पर गुनगुना पानी पीती रहिए। दो-तीन दिन में ही आपको काफ़ी राहत मिल जाएगी।
पल्लवी	क्या मुझे पाँच दिन बाद फिर आना होगा?

डा. भट	यदि आप पाँच दिन की दवा के बाद भी पूरी तरह स्वस्थ न हों तो हमें ख़ून की और फेफड़ों की जाँच करनी होगी। लेकिन मैं नहीं समझता हूँ कि इस की ज़रूरत होगी।
पल्लवी	धन्यवाद, डाक्टर। नमस्ते।

6.4 Consulting a doctor

A cough and a sore throat

Pallavi	Good evening, Doctor.
Dr. Bhat	Have a seat, Mrs. Jain. What seems to be the problem?
Pallavi	I've had a sore throat for several days. My throat hurts and I'm plagued by incessant coughing.
Dr. Bhat	Is it a dry cough or are you coughing up phlegm?
Pallavi	I had a dry cough to begin with, but for the last three days I have been coughing up yellowish phlegm.
Dr. Bhat	How many days has it been since the coughing started?
Pallavi	It's almost ten days now. It was less severe in the beginning, but has been worsening day by day. Now I've started having some trouble breathing as well.
Dr. Bhat	Do you have any symptoms of a cold? A running nose, or fever?
Pallavi	I did, but not any longer. It was with a cold that the cough started. I also had high fever for two days, but that subsided on its own. Now the cold has gone, but I can't seem to get rid of this cough.
Dr. Bhat	Hold your wrist out, I'm going to take your pulse. Now open your mouth, put your tongue out and say "aaah". Does your throat hurt? Now lie down here. Take a deep breath ... yes, once more ... since when have you had this wheezing sound while breathing? Does your chest hurt when I press here?
Pallavi	Not like this, but it does sometimes when I have a bad coughing fit.
Dr. Bhat	You can get up now. I'm going to write you a prescription. You have acute bronchitis.
Pallavi	Good grief!
Dr. Bhat	It's nothing to worry about. There is generally no difficulty in treating this condition. You'll just have to take

antibiotics for five days, because this has turned into a bacterial infection.

Pallavi   The cough really bothers me, Doctor. It ruins my night's sleep.

Dr. Bhat   Yes, the prescription I'm writing contains an expectorant as well. Apart from that, to thin the phlegm you should keep drinking lukewarm water at short intervals. You should get considerable relief from the cough in two or three days.

Pallavi   Will I have to come back in five days?

Dr. Bhat   If you don't recover completely after a five-day course of medicine, we'll need to do a blood test and check your lungs. But I don't think that will be necessary.

Pallavi   Thank you, Doctor. Goodbye.

शब्दावली   Glossary

6.1 बाज़ार में आपात-स्थिति: बेहोश हो जाना
6.1 An emergency in the marketplace: fainting

संभालना   to support, to hold (up)
बेहोश होना   to faint
बेहोशी *f*   unconsciousness, a blackout
अचानक   suddenly, by chance
गिरना   to fall down/to collapse
पंखा *m*   a fan
   पंखा करना   to fan
मुँह *m*   the face
छींटा *m*   a drop
   छींटा डालना   to sprinkle
शांत   quiet, tranquil, peaceful
सामान *m*   goods, provisions
होश *m* आना   to recover consciousness
आराम से   unhurriedly, gently
उठना   to get up, to stand up
धीरे-धीरे   slowly
घबराना/घबड़ाना   to be perturbed/
              agitated
कुर्सी/कुरसी *f*   a chair, a seat
बैठाना/बिठाना   to give a seat/to seat
धूप *f*   sunshine, the heat of the sun
तेज़   strong, hot, burning
छाँह *f*   shade
एकाएक   suddenly, unexpectedly
चक्कर आना   to grow dizzy

पल *m*   a moment, an instant
धड़ाम *m*   any sudden loud sound; thud
   धड़ाम से   with a thud, crash, etc.
डर जाना   to be frightened, get a fright
चोट *f*   a wound, an injury, a bruise
कुहनी *f*   the elbow
ख़ून *m*   blood
बहना   to flow
क्लिनिक *f*   a clinic
इतवार *m*   Sunday
मामूली   ordinary
छिलना   to be scraped or grazed
आख़िर   in the end, after all
कारण *m*   a cause, a reason
ज़ाहिर   evident, apparent
कड़ा   harsh, severe, strong
रक्त *m*   blood
रक्त दबाव *m*   blood pressure
गर्मी/गरमी *f*   heat
पानी की कमी *f*   dehydration
वजह *f*   a cause, a reason
आराम *m* करना   to rest, to relax
हालत *f*   state (of affairs), condition
इंतज़ार *m*   wait, expectation
तकलीफ़ *f*   trouble, difficulty

6.2 घर में आपात-स्थिति: पेट की गड़बड़ी
6.2 An emergency at home: a stomach upset

सहेली *f*   a woman's female friend
तबीयत ख़राब होना   to be/feel unwell

तबीयत *f*   state of health
परेशान   worried, distressed

नज़र आना to come into view, to appear
  नज़र *f* sight, a glance
मुसीबत *f* trouble
बीमार पड़ना to fall ill
रविवार *m* Sunday
ख़राब bad
बुरा bad
पेट *m* the stomach
पेट ख़राब होना to have an upset
                    stomach
उलटी *f* vomiting, nausea
दस्त *m* diarrhoea, dysentry
ऐंठन *f* cramps, colic, griping pain
महसूस होना to be felt
तुरंत quickly, at once
हैज़ा/कॉलेरा *m* cholera
राय *f* advice, opinion
दरवाज़ा *m* a door
खुला to be open
लक्षण *m* a symptom
साफ़ plain, clear
दर्द *m* a pain, an ache
अन्य other, different
तकलीफ़ *f* trouble, difficulty, distress
संख्या *f* a number
बढ़ना to increase, to grow
मतली *f* nausea
रोग *m* an illness, a disease
जी *m* spirits, bodily state
  जी मचलाना/मतलाना to feel nausea

ग़लत wrong
आहार *m* food
आइस-क्रीम *f* ice cream
फ़्रिज *m* a fridge
गड़बड़ *m, f*/गड़बड़ी *f* a disorder
स्पष्ट clear
आहार विषाक्तन *m* food poisoning
शरीर *m* the body
संदूषित contaminated
पदार्थ *m* a product, an object
निकालना to get rid of
कोशिश *f* an effort, an attempt
रोकना to stop, to halt
ख़ुद self (myself, himself, itself, etc.)
ख़तरा *m* danger
लवण *m* salt(s)
पूर्ति *f* 1. the satisfaction of a need, a
            want, etc. 2. the supply of a
            commodity, etc.
घोलना to dissolve
पिलाना to give to drink
थकना to be tired
सुधार *m* an improvement
इलेक्ट्रोलाइट *m* oral rehydration salts,
                    electrolytes
कष्ट *m* an inconvenience, trouble
क़दम *m* a step, a pace
दो/चार क़दम पर a stone's throw from
दूरी *f* a distance
दवा *f* a medicine

6.3 औषधालय/दवाखाने में: दवाएँ ख़रीदना
6.3 At the chemist's: buying medicine

औषधालय/दवा-ख़ाना *m* a chemist,
                         a pharmacy
औषधि/ दवा *f* a medicine
सेवा *f* service

पैकेट/ पैकिट *m* a packet, a parcel
पाउच *m* a small bag, a sachet
थैली *f* a small bag, a sachet
फ़ायदा *m* an advantage, a benefit

पाउडर *m*　a powder
नापना　to measure
लिटर *m*　a litre
सिर-दर्द *m*　a headache
गोली *f*　a tablet, a pill
पत्ता *m*/ पत्ती *f*　a strip
असरदार　effective
मच्छर *m*　a mosquito
भगाना　to chase away
लोशन *m*　a lotion
लेप *m*　an ointment
निहायत　extremely, exceedingly
हाल में　recently
पदार्थ *m*　a product, an object
बदबूदार　stinking, smelling
बदबू *f*　a bad smell, stench
चिपचिपा　sticky, clinging

सुधरना　to improve
टीवी *m*　a TV
विज्ञापान *m*　an advertisement
क्रीम *f*　a cream, an ointment
सुगंधित/ख़ुशबूदार　perfumed, fragrant
सुगंध/ख़ुशबू *f*　fragrance, a sweet smell
इस्तेमाल *m*　use, exercise
इस्तेमाल करना　to use
अक्सर　often
बीवी *f*　a wife
बच्ची *f*　a little girl, a baby girl
चेहरा *m*　the face, the features
त्वचा *f*　the skin
नुक़सान *m*　harm, damage
नुक़सान पहुँचाना/करना　to do damage, to
　　　　　　　　　　harm, to destroy
उम्मीद *f*　hope, expectation
परखना　to judge, to test

6.4 डाक्टर से परामर्श करना: खाँसी, गला ख़राब होना
6.4 Consulting a doctor: a cough and a sore throat

परामर्श *m*　advice, consultation
ख़ाँसी *f*　a cough
गला *m*　1. the throat 2. the neck
गला ख़राब होना　to have a sore throat
तकलीफ़ *f*　trouble, difficulty, distress
ख़ाँसना　to cough
सूखा　dry
बलग़म *m*　phlegm, mucus
पीला-सा　yellowish
बदतर　worse
साँस *f*　a breath
　साँस लेना　to breathe, to draw breath
जुकाम *m*　a cold
नाक *f*　the nose
　नाक बहना　*nose*: to run

लंबा　long
आवाज़ *f*　a sound
बुख़ार *m*　a fever
तेज़　high
आप से आप　of its own accord
उतरना　to come down, to sink/subside
छुटकारा *m*　relief, release
　छुटकारा मिलना　to be freed, to get rid of
कलाई *f*　the wrist
नाड़ी *f*　the pulse
मुँह *m*　the mouth
ख़ोलना　to open
जीभ *f*　the tongue
लेटना　to lie down
दबाना　to press

छाती *f* the chest

ज़ोर *m* strength, force

ज़ोर से severely, violently

दौरा *m* a fit, an attack (of illness, etc.)

नुसख़ा *m* a prescription

तीव्र acute, strong, intense

ब्रांकाइटिस *f* bronchitis

चिंता *f* concern, anxiety, worry

इलाज *m* 1. a remedy, a cure
       2. treatment

कठिनाई *f* a difficulty

ऐंटीबायोटिक *m* an antibiotic

जीवाणु *m* bacteria

बैक्टीरियल bacterial

संक्रमण *m* an infection

तंग करना to distress, to trouble

नींद *f* sleep

पतला thin

गुनगुना lukewarm, tepid

राहत *f* relief

स्वस्थ healthy

स्वस्थ हो जाना to recover

फेफड़ा *m* the lung

जाँच *f* an examination

7
नाते-रिश्ते
Family relations

7.1   **परिवार में**

 24

रिश्तेदारों से मिलना

अश्रान्त   नमस्कार, चाचीजी।

पल्लवी   अरे, अश्रान्त बेटे! नमस्ते, आओ, अन्दर आओ!। बैठो, बेटा। अरसे से
            तुम्हें देखा नहीं। (पुकार कर) राजन! देखो कौन आया है!

अश्रान्त   नमस्ते, राजन चाचा।

राजन   अरे वाह, अश्रान्त है! तुम तो बिलकुल ईद का चाँद हो गए हो, कहाँ रहते
            हो?

अश्रान्त	मैं बहुत व्यस्त था इसलिए इतने दिन मिलने नहीं आ पाया। बात यह है कि हमारी कंपनी को छह महीने पहले अमेरिका से एक बहुत बड़ा प्रॉजेक्ट मिला था। तब से हम लोग रात-दिन एक कर के उसी में लगे हुए हैं।
पल्लवी	तुम बिलकुल ठीक समय पर आए हो। नाइता तैयार है, आओ साथ बैठ कर नाइता करो।
अश्रान्त	क्षमा कीजिएगा, चाचीजी, मुझे एक घंटे में एक मीटिंग में पहुँचना है।
राजन	अरे बेटा, तुम्हारे लिए छुट्टी और आराम नाम की कोई चीज़ नहीं होती?
पल्लवी	एकदम सही नाम पड़ा है — तुम सच में कभी थकते नहीं हो! चलो, कम से कम हमारे साथ चाय तो पी लो।
राजन	अच्छा बताओ, आज सवेरे-सवेरे कैसे आना हुआ? और यह लड्डू किस उपलक्ष्य में हैं?
अश्रान्त	एक ख़ुशख़बरी देनी है। मैंने सोचा कि आप लोगों का आशीर्वाद ले लूँ और मुँह मीठा कर दूँ।
राजन	जीते रहो, बेटे। लेकिन शुभ समाचार तो सुनाओ!
पल्लवी	शुभाशीष, अश्रान्त बेटा। बात पक्की हो गई?
अश्रान्त	जी, चाचीजी।
पल्लवी	तुम ने तो सुबह-सुबह ही मन प्रसन्न कर दिया! तो बताओ, कौन है वह भाग्यशाली लड़की?
अश्रान्त	लड़की? आप किस बात का ज़िक्र कर रही हैं?
पल्लवी	तुम्हारी शादी का, और क्या? शर्माओ मत, तुम्हारी माँ ने मुझे बता दिया था कि तुम्हारे लिए बहुत अच्छे रिश्ते आ रहे हैं। और तुम ने अभी-अभी तो कहा कि बात पक्की हो गई है।
अश्रान्त	अरे, चाचीजी, मैं शादी की नहीं, नौकरी की बात कर रहा था।
पल्लवी	नौकरी की?
अश्रान्त	जी हाँ, अमरीका वाले प्रॉजेक्ट का काम संभालने के लिए मेरी कंपनी मुझे न्यू यॉर्क भेज रही है।
राजन	शाबाश बेटे! यह तो ख़ूब बढ़िया समाचार है। कब जाना है?
अश्रान्त	दो-तीन महीने बाद ही।
पल्लवी	बहुत बहुत बधाई हो। कितने दिन के लिए जाओगे?
अश्रान्त	कम से कम तीन साल के लिए।
पल्लवी	इतना लंबा अरसा! और तुम अकेले जाओगे? अपने परिवार और दोस्तों से इतनी दूर वहाँ एकदम अकेले पड़ जाओगे।
अश्रान्त	आप ठीक कह रही हैं, चाचीजी, लेकिन क्या करूँ? मुझे काम में उन्नति करने का बहुत बड़ा मौका मिल रहा है, लेकिन इतनी जल्दी मेरे साथ

	विदेश चल देने को भला कौन-सी लड़की तैयार होगी? वैसे भी अम्मा को कोई लड़की पसंद ही नहीं आती।
राजन	बात तो सही है। रिश्ता पक्का करने का काम जल्दबाज़ी में नहीं करना चाहिए। आख़िर पूरे जीवन के साथ का सवाल होता है। देखो न, मुझे उस समय तो पल्लवी से शादी करने की जल्दी पड़ी थी, लेकिन अब कितना पछता रहा हूँ!
पल्लवी	अच्छा, तो पछता रहे हो तुम! तो फिर देखते जाओ, मैं अभी कितना और सताती हूँ!
अश्रान्त	आप लोगों के साथ हँसी-मज़ाक में सचमुच बहुत मज़ा आता है। लेकिन अब मुझे निकलना चाहिए नहीं तो मीटिंग में देर से पहुँचूँगा। नमस्ते।
राजन	ख़ुश रहो। आते रहना।
पल्लवी	और भैया-भाभी से हमारा प्रणाम कहना।

7.1   In the family

Meeting relatives

Ashrant	Good morning, Aunty.
Pallavi	Ah, Ashrant, my boy! Good morning, come in, come in! Have a seat, son. Haven't seen you for ages. (Calling) Rajan! Look who's here!
Ashrant	Hello, Uncle Rajan.
Rajan	Oh, great, it's Ashrant! You're a rare sight in these parts, where have you been keeping yourself?
Ashrant	I've been very busy, that's why I couldn't come and visit. The thing is, our company got this huge project from America six months ago, and we've been working on it day and night since then.
Pallavi	You've arrived at just the right time. Breakfast is ready, come and sit down and have some with us.
Ashrant	I'm sorry, Aunty, but I've to get to a meeting in an hour.
Rajan	Now now, my boy, have holidays and leisure no meaning at all for you?
Pallavi	Your name suits you perfectly – you really are tireless! Come, have some tea with us at least.
Rajan	Now tell us, what brings you here at this early morning hour? And what are the sweets in honour of?

Ashrant	I have a bit of good news. I thought I'd ask for your blessings and celebrate the occasion with these sweets.
Rajan	May you live long, my boy. But do tell us the good news.
Pallavi	My blessings, dear Ashrant. So is the matter settled?
Ashrant	Yes, aunty.
Pallavi	You've really given us something to rejoice over early in the moning. So tell us, who's the lucky girl?
Ashrant	Girl? What are you talking about?
Pallavi	About your getting married, what else? You don't have to feel embarrassed, your mother had told me that some very good proposals of marriage have been coming in for you. And you just said that the matter had been settled.
Ashrant	Oh no, Aunty, I wasn't talking about marriage, I was talking about my job.
Pallavi	About your job?
Ashrant	Yes, my company is sending me to New York to look after the American project.
Rajan	Well done, son! That's splendid news. When do you have to leave?
Ashrant	In just two or three months.
Pallavi	Congratulations! For how long will you go?
Ashrant	For at least three years.
Pallavi	Such a long time! And will you go alone? You're going to get lonesome without your family and friends.
Ashrant	What you're saying is quite right, Aunty, but what can I do? I'm getting such a good opportunity to get ahead in my job, but what girl would ever agree to go off abroad with me at such short notice? Anyway, Mum never likes any of the girls.
Rajan	And quite right, too. Arranging a match is not something that should be done in haste. After all, it's a question of a lifelong commitment. Look at me, I was in such a hurry to marry Pallavi then, but how much I'm regretting it now!
Pallavi	Aha, so you regret it, do you? Then wait and see how much more I'll torment you!
Ashrant	Your laughter and joviality is always so much fun. But I should be leaving now, or else I'll be late for my meeting. Bye!
Rajan	Bless you. Do drop by sometimes.
Pallavi	And give our regards to your parents.

7.2   संयुक्त परिवार से भेंट

रिश्तेदार ही रिश्तेदार

पल्लवी	अरे, अलका, आज तो तुम्हारे घर में सन्नाटा छाया हुआ है! बच्चे कहाँ हैं?
अलका	मेरे सास-ससुर बच्चों को घुमाने ले गए हैं। अब शाम को खाना-वाना खाने के बाद ही लौटेंगे।
पल्लवी	कितनी अच्छी बात है कि तुम्हारी ससुराल दिल्ली में ही है — दादा-दादी और पोते मिलते रहते हैं।
अलका	हाँ, और मेरा मायका भी दूर नहीं है। बच्चे अक्सर जयपुर जाकर नाना-नानी तथा और भी ढेर-से संबंधियों से भी मिल लेते हैं।
पल्लवी	जयपुर में तो तुम्हारे बेटों को बहुत ही मज़ा आता होगा क्योंकि तुम्हारा परिवार इतना बड़ा है। वहाँ बच्चों को लाड़-प्यार से बिगाड़ने के लिए उनके मामा, मौसी और अनेक लोग हैं।
अलका	तुम तो मेरे परिवार के बहुत से सदस्यों से मिल चुकी हो, न? देखो, हम लोगों की यह फ़ोटो हाल में शादी में ली गई थी।
पल्लवी	कितनी सुंदर फ़ोटो है! लेकिन इस में ऐसे भी कुछ लोग हैं जिन्हें मैं जानती नहीं। ज़रा देखूँ … यह तो तुम्हारे माँ और पिताजी हैं, उनके बगल में तुम्हारे दोनों चाचा-चाची, फिर उनके बेटे, यानी तुम्हारे चचेरे भाई। लेकिन ये कौन हैं? इन्हे मैंने पहचाना नहीं।
अलका	मेरी बड़ी बुआ हैं जो इलाहाबाद में रहती हैं। फूफाजी का देहांत हो चुका है। बुआजी के पास उनका बेटा, बहू और पोती खड़े हैं।
पल्लवी	तुम्हारे सगे भाइयों और भाभियों को तो मैं अच्छी तरह जानती हूँ, और तुम्हारी दीदी और जीजाजी को भी। सब के बच्चे इतने बड़े हो गए हैं कि पहचान में ही नहीं आते! यह तुम्हारी बड़ी बहन की बेटी है, न? कितनी सुंदर हो गई है!
अलका	हाँ, यह मेरी भानजी नयनतारा है। कमाल की लड़की है। सुंदर तो है ही, इतनी हँसमुख और मिलनसार है कि सब का मन मोह लेती है। यही नहीं, अक़्लमंद भी है। बहुत जाने-माने अमरीकी विश्वविद्यालय में उसे एम.ए. करने के लिए छात्रवृति मिली थी। और अब पी.एच.डी. करने की भी।
पल्लवी	पढ़ती क्या है वह?
अलका	अर्थ-शास्त्र। चलो पल्लवी, चाय पी जाए। रसोई में चलें? मैं गरम-गरम चाय बनाती हूँ।

7.2   Getting to know a joint family

Relatives galore

Pallavi	Hey, Alka, there's absolute silence in your house today! Where are the children?
Alka	My parents-in-law have taken them on an outing. They'll come back only in the evening now, after they've had dinner and all.
Pallavi	How nice it is that your in-laws live right here in Delhi – the grandparents and grandsons can keep seeing each other.
Alka	Yes, and my parents' home isn't too far away, either. The children often go to Jaipur and meet the other grandparents and a whole lot of other relatives as well.
Pallavi	Your sons must really enjoy going to Jaipur because your family is so big. Their uncle, aunt and a lot of other people are there to pamper them with their affection.
Alka	You've met many of my family members, haven't you? Look, this photograph of ours was taken recently at a wedding.
Pallavi	What a lovely photo! But there are some people in it whom I don't know. Let me see ... these are your mother and father, and both your uncles next to them, then their sons, your cousins, that is. But who's this? I don't recognize her.
Alka	That's my aunt, my father's elder sister who lives in Allahabad. My uncle has passed away. Aunty's son, daughter-in-law and granddaughter are standing beside her.
Pallavi	I know your brothers and their wives very well, of course, and your sister and her husband, too. All their children are so grown up now that it's hard to recognize them. This is your elder sister's daughter, isn't she? How pretty she's become!
Alka	Yes, that's my niece, Nayantara. She's a wonderful girl. Not only is she pretty, she's such a cheerful and friendly person that everybody's charmed by her. And not only that, she's highly intelligent, too. She won a scholarship to a prestigious American university to do her master's. And now she's got one to do a PhD as well.
Pallavi	And what's she studying?
Alka	Economics. Come, Pallavi, let's have some tea. Shall we go to the kitchen? I'll make us some nice hot tea.

7.3 शादी तय करना

 रिश्ता जोड़ना

पल्लवी	तुम अपनी भानजी नयनतारा के बारे में बता रही थीं। ऐसी गुणी बेटी पर उस के माँ-बाप को बहुत गर्व होगा।
अलका	माँ-बाप तो उस पर जान देते हैं लेकिन मेरे जीजा के घरवाले उस से बहुत अप्रसन्न हैं। वे लोग भी संयुक्त परिवार में रहते हैं और नयनतारा की वजह से उन के घर में हर समय किच-किच चलती रहती है।
पल्लवी	अरे, ऐसा क्यों?
अलका	घरवाले काफ़ी रूढ़िवादी विचार के हैं। वे नयनतारा की शादी करवाने की रट लगाए हैं। कहते हैं कि इतनी पढ़ाई-लिखाई का लाभ ही क्या हुआ जब लड़की छब्बीस साल की उम्र में भी कुँवारी है।
पल्लवी	तो क्या नयनतारा शादी करना ही नहीं चाहती? या हो सकता है कि उस ने अमरीका में ही किसी को पसंद कर लिया हो।
अलका	नहीं, ऐसी कोई बात नहीं है। लेकिन वह मन लगा कर पढ़ती है और अपने शोध-कार्य के लिए अमरीका में दो-तीन वर्ष और रहना चाहती है। आख़िर कोलंबिया युनिवर्सिटी से डाक्टर की उपाधि प्राप्त करना कोई ऐसी-वैसी बात थोड़े ही है!
पल्लवी	क्या कहा तुमने? कोलंबिया? वही विश्वविद्यालय जो न्यू यॉर्क में है?
अलका	हाँ, वही।
पल्लवी	न्यू यॉर्क! कैसा संयोग है! वाह, क्या जोड़ी बनेगी!
अलका	संयोग? जोड़ी? तुम तो पहेलियाँ बुझा रही हो, पल्लवी।
पल्लवी	मुझे सब की समस्याओं का समाधान करने का एक रास्ता दिख रहा है। सुनो। तुम मेरे भतीजे अश्रांत को जानती हो, न?
अलका	हाँ, अच्छी तरह से। बहुत समझदार और सुशील लड़का है।
पल्लवी	उस के माँ-बाप, यानी मेरे जेठ और जिठानी, उस के लिए लड़की ढूंढ रहे हैं। रिश्ता जल्दी से जल्दी तय हो जाना चाहिए। तो बताओ, तुम्हारी नयनतारा और मेरे अश्रांत की जोड़ी कैसी रहेगी?
अलका	मेल तो दोनों का बढ़िया बैठेगा, लेकिन अश्रांत की तो दिल्ली में बहुत अच्छी नौकरी है, और नयनतारा अभी न्यू यॉर्क में रहना चाहती है।
पल्लवी	यही तो संयोग की बात है! अश्रांत की तीन-चार साल के लिए न्यू यॉर्क में बदली होने वाली है।

अलका   सच? तब तो हमें ज़रा भी देर नहीं करनी चाहिए! तुम अपने धरवालों से
       बात करो और मैं अपने लोगों को यह सुझाव देती हूँ।
पल्लवी अगर दोनों बच्चे एक-दूसरे को पसंद कर लें तो कितना अच्छा रहेगा!
अलका   सोचो तो — फिर हम दोनों की दोस्ती रिश्तेदारी में बदल जाएगी!

7.3   Arranging a marriage

Matchmaking

Pallavi	You were talking about your niece, Nayantara. Her parents must be proud to have such a talented daughter.
Alka	Her parents absolutely dote on her, but my brother-in-law's family are very displeased with her. They live in an extended family, too, and there's constant wrangling in the house because of Nayantara.
Pallavi	Really? Why's that?
Alka	The family have fairly conservative views. All they talk about is getting Nayanatra married. They say, what's the point of so much education if the girl is still not married at the age of 26?
Pallavi	So doesn't Nayantara wish to marry at all? Or maybe she's found someone for herself in America already.
Alka	No, it's nothing of the sort. But she studies with total dedication and wants to stay on in the States for another two or three years to do her research work. After all, it's no mean achievement to get a doctorate from Columbia University!
Pallavi	What did you say? Columbia? The university that's in New York?
Alka	Yes, that's the one.
Pallavi	New York! What a coincidence! What a perfect couple they'll make!
Alka	Coincidence? Couple? You're talking in riddles, Pallavi!
Pallavi	I can see a way of solving everybody's problems. Listen. You know my nephew, Ashrant, don't you?
Alka	Yes, very well. He's a very sensible and decent boy.
Pallavi	His parents, that is, my brother-in-law and his wife, are looking for a suitable girl for him. A match needs to be arranged as soon as possible. So tell me, do you think your Nayantara and my Ashrant would be right for each other?

Alka	I think they'd make a perfect match, but Ashrant has a very good job in Delhi and Nayantara wants to stay in New York for the present.
Pallavi	That's just what the coincidence is! Ashrant is going to be transferred to New York for three to four years.
Alka	Really? Then we shouldn't delay the matter at all! You talk to your relatives and I'll suggest this to my people.
Pallavi	How wonderful it will be if both the children like each other!
Alka	Just imagine – our friendship will then turn into a family relationship!

शब्दावली   Glossary

7.1 परिवार में: रिश्तेदारों से मिलना
7.1 In the family: meeting relatives

परिवार *m* a family
रिश्तेदार *m* a relative
अरसा *m* a space of time, an interval
  अरसे से for a long (past) time
पुकारना to call out
चाचा *m* an uncle (father's younger
      brother)
चाची *f* an aunt (father's younger
      brother's wife)
ईद *f* Id/Eid, a Muslim holiday that
    marks the end of the Islamic
    holy month of fasting, Ramadan
  ईद का चाँद something/someone
        rarely seen
चाँद *m* the moon
व्यस्त occupied, busy
रात–दिन एक करना to work night and day
नाश्ता *m* breakfast
तैयार ready
क्षमा *f* forgiveness
मीटिंग *f* a meeting
आराम *m* rest, ease, comfort
थकना to be tired
अश्रांत tireless
उपलक्ष्य *m* an occasion
ख़ुशख़बरी *f* good news
आशीर्वाद *m* blessing
मुँह मीठा करना to give sweets (in cele-
        bration of a happy event)
जीते रहो may you have a long life!
शुभ auspicious
समाचार *m* news
शुभाशीष *m* blessing
पक्का finalised, definite

बात पक्की होना to be a settled matter
मन *m* the mind/the heart/the soul
प्रसन्न pleased, delighted
भाग्यशाली lucky, fortunate
लड़की *f* 1. a girl 2. a future wife
ज़िक्र *m* mention
शादी *f* marriage
शर्माना / शरमाना to be embarrassed
रिश्ता *m* a relationship, an alliance
  रिश्ता आना to receive a proposal of
        marriage
नौकरी *f* work, employment
शाबाश Well done! Splendid!
बधाई *f* congratulation(s)
अकेले पड़ना to grow lonely
उन्नति *f* advance, progress
मौका *m* a chance, an opportunity
भला indeed, in truth
रिश्ता पक्का करना to arrange a marriage
जल्दबाज़ी *f* haste, hurry, impetuosity
पूरा whole, complete
जीवन *m* life
साथ *m* 1. company 2. a close bond
सवाल *m* a question, a matter
जल्दी पड़ी होना to be in a hurry
पछताना to repent, to regret
सताना to torment, to torture
हँसी–मज़ाक *f* laughing and joking,
        joviality
ख़ुश रहो may you always be happy!
भैया *m* an (elder) brother
भाभी *m* a sister-in-law (brother's
      wife)
प्रणाम *m* a respectful greeting

7.2 संयुक्त परिवार से भेंट: रिश्तेदार ही रिश्तेदार
7.2 Getting to know a joint family: relatives galore

संयुक्त   joint

सन्नाटा *m*   a dead silence, stillness

छाना   to be spread

सास *f*   a mother-in-law

ससुर *m*   a father-in-law

घुमाना   to take someone out/round

ससुराल *f*   father-in-law's house or
   family

दादा *m*   a paternal grandfather

दादी *f*   a paternal grandmother

पोता *m*   a grandson (son's son)

पोती *f*   a granddaughter (son's
   daughter)

मायका *m*   mother's house, parental
   home (of a married woman)

नाना *m*   a maternal grandfather

नानी *f*   a maternal grandmother

ढेर-से   a great number, many

संबंधी *m*   a relative

लाड़-प्यार *m*   love and affection

बिगाड़ना   to pamper, to spoil

मामा *m*   a maternal uncle

मामी *f*   an aunt (maternal uncle's wife)

मौसी *f*   a maternal aunt

मौसा *m*   an uncle (maternal aunt's
   husband)

अनेक   several

सदस्य *m*   a member

सुंदर   beautiful

माँ *f*   a mother

पिता *m*   a father

सगा   born of the same parents

चचेरा भाई *m*   a cousin (father's
   brother's son)

बड़ा   elder, older

बुआ / फूफी *f*   an aunt (father's sister)

फूफाजी *m*   an uncle (father's sister's
   husband)

देहांत *m*   death

बहू *f*   a daughter-in-law

दीदी / जीजी *f*   an elder sister

जीजाजी *m*   a brother-in-law (elder
   sister's husband)

भानजा / भांजा *m*   a nephew (sister's son)

भानजी / भांजी *f*   a niece (sister's
   daughter)

कमाल *m*   a miracle, a wonderful thing

कमाल का   wonderful

हँसमुख   cheerful

मिलनसार   sociable, friendly, affable

मन मोहना   to captivate, to charm

अक़्लमंद   intelligent

एम.ए. *m*   MA, a master's degree

छात्रवृति *f*   a scholarship

पी.एच.डी. *m*   PhD, a doctorate

पढ़ाई *f*   study

विषय *m*   a subject

अर्थ-शास्त्र *m*   economics

7.3 शादी तय करना: रिश्ता जोड़ना
7.3 Arranging a marriage: matchmaking

गुणी talented, excellent, worthy
गर्व *m* pride
(पर) जान देना to dote (on/upon), to be very devoted (to)
घरवाले *pl* family, family members
अप्रसन्न displeased
किच-किच *f* wrangling
रूढ़िवादी conservative, traditional
विचार *m* an opinion, a view
शादी करवाना to get someone married
रट *f* repetition
रट लगाना to repeat ad nauseam
लाभ *m* a benefit, an advantage, gain
उम्र *f* age
कुँवारी /कुँआरी *f* an unmarried woman
पसंद करना to like, to choose
(में) मन लगाना to devote oneself (to), to concentrate (on)
पढ़ना to study
शोध-कार्य *m* research work
वर्ष *m* a year
उपाधि *f* a title, a degree
प्राप्त करना to obtain
ऐसा-वैसा nondescript, commonplace

थोड़े ही hardly
जोड़ी बनना to make a good couple
संयोग *m* a coincidence
पहेली *f* a riddle
  पहेलियाँ बुझाना to speak in riddles
समस्या *f* a problem
समाधान *m* a solution (of a problem)
रास्ता *m* a way, a solution (to a problem)
दिखना to be visible
भतीजा *m* a nephew (brother's son)
भतीजी *f* a niece (brother's daughter)
समझदार intelligent, discerning
सुशील of good character or disposition
जेठ *m* a brother-in-law (husband's elder brother)
जिठानी /जेठानी *f* a sister-in-law (wife of husband's elder brother)
जोड़ी *f*/जोड़ा *m* a couple, a pair
मेल बैठना to be compatible, to harmonise
बदली *f* a transfer
सुझाव *m* a suggestion
बदलना to change, to be transformed

8
तीज-त्योहार, धम-कर्म
Festivals and religious rites

8.1   दीपावली का पर्व

दीपों की रोशनी का त्योहार

अजय	आप लोगों के यहाँ बड़े ज़ोर-शोर से सफ़ाई हो रही है, पल्लवी जी! क्या दीवाली की तैयारियाँ चल रही हैं?
पल्लवी	हाँ, त्योहार के बहाने कम से कम साल में एक बार तो घर ठीक से साफ़ हो जाता है।
आन्या	कई लोगों के घरों में पुताई भी हो रही है। क्या इस का भी दीवाली से संबंध है?
अजय	हाँ, यह एक पुरानी प्रथा है। दीवाली में महालक्ष्मी को पूजा जाता है और उन का स्वागत करने के लिए लोग अपने-अपने घरों को सजाते और साफ़

	करते हैं। व्यापारी लोग भी दीवाली से पहले अपनी दुकानों की सफ़ाई और सजावट करते हैं।
पल्लवी	माना यह जाता है कि लक्ष्मी केवल स्वच्छ स्थानों में प्रवेश करती हैं। और यह तो सभी चाहते हैं कि देवी उनके घर आएँ।
आन्या	लक्ष्मी धन-दौलत की देवी हैं, न?
अजय	हाँ, उनकी और उनके साथ गणेश की पूजा कर के लोग आने वाले वर्ष के लिये सुख, संपत्ति और सफलता की कामना करते हैं।
पल्लवी	मूल रूप में दीपावली रोशनी का उत्सव है। छोटी-सी कुटिया हो चाहे आलीशान महल, पर्व के दिन सभी घर बत्तियों से उज्ज्वलित होते हैं।
आन्या	दीपक जलाने का क्या महत्त्व है? मेरा मतलब है, दीवाली मनाते क्यों है?
अजय	दीवाली कार्तिक की अमावस्या पर पड़ती है। अंधेरी रात में अनगिनत दीपों का जगमगाना तमस् के ऊपर ज्योति की जीत का प्रतीक है।
पल्लवी	उत्तर भारत में हम लोग मानते हैं कि रामचंद्रजी इसी दिन चौदह वर्ष के वनवास के बाद विजयी होकर अयोध्या लौटे थे। इसी की खुशी में हम दीये जलाते हैं। लेकिन हर प्रांत की कहानी थोड़ी अलग होती है।
आन्या	तो यह सिर्फ़ उत्तर भारत का पर्व नहीं है?
अजय	नहीं, भारत के सभी भागों के हिंदु किसी न किसी रूप में दीवाली मनाते हैं। इस उत्सव की उमंग पूरे देश में फैली होती है।

8.1   Deepawali

The festival of lights

Ajay	Your place is being cleaned with great fervour, Pallavi-ji! Are preparations for Diwali in progress?
Pallavi	Yes, the festival provides an excuse for getting the house cleaned up properly once a year at least.
Anja	Several people are having their homes whitewashed. Is that too connected with Diwali?
Ajay	Yes, it's a traditional custom. The goddess Laxmi is worshipped during Diwali and, to welcome her, people clean and decorate their homes. Shopkeepers, too, clean out and decorate their shops.
Pallavi	It is believed that Laxmi enters only places that are spotlessly clean. And of course everyone wants the goddess to visit their home.

Anja	Laxmi is the goddess of wealth, isn't she?
Ajay	That's right, and by offering prayers to her as well as to Ganesh, people wish for happiness, prosperity and success in the coming year.
Pallavi	Diwali is basically a celebration of light. Whether it's a tiny hut or a magnificent palace, all homes are ablaze with lights on the day of the festival.
Anja	What is the significance of lighting lamps? I mean, why is Diwali celebrated?
Ajay	Diwali falls on new moon in the month of Kartik. The twinkling of countless lamps in the dark night symbolises the triumph of good over evil.
Pallavi	In North India, we believe that on this day, Lord Rama returned victorious to Ayodhya after 14 years spent in exile in the forest. We light lamps in celebration of this happy event. But every region has its own slightly different story.
Anja	So this is not just a North Indian festival?
Ajay	No, Hindus in every part of India celebrate Diwali in one way or another. The joyous spirit of the festival pervades the whole country.

8.2　दीवाली मनाना

कुछ प्रथाएँ

आन्या	पल्लवी जी, आप की बेटियाँ त्योहार के लिए पुणे से आएँगी कि वे अपने कॉलज में ही दीवाली मनाती हैं?
पल्लवी	घर तो अवश्य आएँगी। स्कूलों और विश्वविद्यालयों में दीवाली की छुट्टियाँ होती हैं – यह पर्व परिवार और संबंधियों के साथ जो मनाया जाता है।
आन्या	आप लोग दीवाली का त्योहार कैसे मनाते हैं?
पल्लवी	हमारी तैयारियाँ तो काफ़ी पहले से ही शुरू हो जाती हैं। घर की साफ़-सफ़ाई के अलावा ज़ोर-शोर से ख़रीदारी भी होती है, ख़ास तौर पर कपड़ों की क्योंकि दीवाली के उत्सव पर सुंदर नए कपड़े पहनने का रिवाज़ है। दीवाली पूजा के लिए हम लोग लक्ष्मी और गणेशजी की मिट्टी की मूर्तियाँ भी ख़रीदते हैं।

आन्या	तालकटोरा मैदान के पास जो बड़ा-सा दीवाली मेला लगा है, वहाँ में कल गई थी। वहाँ ख़ूबसूरत हस्तशिल्प की वस्तुएँ बिक रही हैं।
पल्लवी	हाँ, दीवाली मेलों की सैर करके पर्व के लिए दीये, मोमबत्तियाँ, पटाके, मिठाइयाँ वग़ैरह ख़रीदना — इस सब की वजह से पहले से ही रौनक़ हो जाती है। ख़ासकर बच्चे इस त्योहार का बेचैनी से इंतज़ार करते हैं।
अजय	मुझे बचपन में दीवाली बेहद पसंद थी क्योंकि इस अवसर पर घर में ढेर-से पकवान बना करते थे और हमें तरह-तरह की मिठाइयाँ खाने को मिलती थीं।
पल्लवी	जी हाँ, बिना मिठाइयों के क्या दीवाली! इन्हें रिश्तेदारों और दोस्तों को बाँटना भी इस त्योहार की प्रथा है।
आन्या	अच्छा, इसी लिए मिठाई की दुकानों में आजकल भीड़ लगी रहती है!
पल्लवी	दीवाली पर सुबह से ही महमानों का आना-जाना और आपस में मिठाइयाँ और शुभकामनाएँ बाँटना शुरू हो जाता है। सवेरे-सवेरे ही मेरी बेटियाँ दरवाज़े पर रंगोली बनाती हैं। फिर हम लोग घर के इर्द-गिर्द दीये सजाते हैं जिन्हें शाम को जलाते हैं।
आन्या	और पूजा? वह शाम को होती है?
पल्लवी	जी। सूरज डूबने पर हम चारों लक्ष्मी और गणेश जी की मूर्तियों के सामने दिये जलाकर उन को फूल और नैवेद्य चढ़ाकर पूजते हैं। पूजा के बाद पूरे घर के दीये जलाए जाते हैं।
अजय	आप लोग आतिशबाज़ी नहीं जलाते?
पल्लवी	जब बच्चे छोटे थे तो उन्हें फुलझड़ी और अनार जलाने का शौक़ था, पर अब प्रदूषण का लिहाज़ करके पटाके नहीं जलाते। लेकिन आस-पास की सज्जा और आतिशबाज़ी देखने हम लोग मोहल्ले में टहल आते हैं।
आन्या	यह मेरी भारत में पहली दीपावली होगी। मैं भी बच्चों की तरह बहुत उत्सुकता से उस की इंतज़ारी कर रही हूँ!

8.2   Celebrating Diwali

Some customs

Anja	Pallavi-ji, are your daughters coming from Pune for the festival or do they celebrate Diwali in college there?
Pallavi	They're most certainly coming. Schools and universities have Diwali holidays – this festival is celebrated with family and relatives.

Anja	And how do you celebrate Diwali?
Pallavi	Our preparations start quite early. Apart from spring-cleaning the flat, we shop with great gusto, especially for clothes, because of the custom of wearing nice new clothes on the occasion of Diwali. We also buy clay figurines of Laxmi and Ganesh for the ceremonial Diwali prayers,
Anja	Yesterday I went to the big Diwali fair which is on near the Talkatora ground. There are beautiful handicrafts on sale there.
Pallavi	Yes, strolling around the Diwali markets and buying lamps, candles, firecrackers, sweets and so on – all this creates an atmosphere of excited anticipation. Children especially wait very impatiently for this festival.
Ajay	I used to love Diwali as a child because so many tasty treats were prepared for the occasion and we got to eat a great variety of sweets.
Pallavi	True, what would Diwali be without sweets! Presenting sweets to relatives and friends is also a Diwali tradition.
Anja	Oh, I see, so that is why there are such large crowds in the sweet shops these days!
Pallavi	On Diwali day, the coming and going of visitors and the mutual exchange of sweets and greetings begins in the morning already. Early in the morning, my daughters make decorative floor paintings at the front door. Then we all place lamps all around the house which we light in the evening.
Anja	And the prayer? Is that performed in the evening?
Pallavi	Yes. At sunset, all of us light lamps before the statues of Laxmi and Ganesh and make a ritual offering of flowers and fruit to them. After the prayers, we light the lamps in the whole house.
Ajay	Don't you set off any fireworks?
Pallavi	The children were fond of sparklers and Bengal lights when they were young, but now we've stopped setting off firecrackers in view of air pollution. But we take a stroll around the neighbourhood to take a look at the decorations and firework displays around us.
Anja	This will be my first Diwali in India. I'm looking forward to it as eagerly as a child!

8.3 मंदिर के दर्शन

संध्या की आरती

राजन	आन्या, आप ने लक्ष्मीनारायण मंदिर अभी तक देखा नहीं है?
आन्या	जी नहीं। मुझे अपने साथ ले चलने के लिए आप का बहुत धन्यवाद।
पल्लवी	दीवाली और जन्माष्टमी पर यह मंदिर खचाखच भरा रहता है। शुक्र है कि दीवाली के अभी बारह दिन बाकी हैं!
आन्या	मुझे अंदर तो जाने दिया जाएगा न, हालाँकि मैं हिन्दु नहीं हूँ?
पल्लवी	हाँ, हाँ, क्यों नहीं। हमारे देश में हर धर्म के लोग हर देव-स्थान में जा सकते हैं, चाहे वह मंदिर हो या मस्जिद या गिरजाघर।
आन्या	लेकिन दक्षिण भारत में और उड़ीसा में भी मैंने ऐसे मंदिर देखे हैं जिनमें ग़ैर-हिन्दुओं का जाना मना है।
राजन	बात तो आप की सही है लेकिन ऐसे मंदिर कम ही होते हैं। देखिए, हम पहुँच गए। पल्लवी, तुम्हें फूल चढ़ाने हैं?
पल्लवी	हाँ, मैं ज़रा फूल ख़रीद लूँ। आन्या, आप के लिए भी?
राजन	अन्दर जाने से पहले जूते-चप्पल उतार कर यहाँ रखने पड़ेंगे।
आन्या	अरे, कितनी बड़ी और शांत जगह है यह! यहाँ एक मंदिर ही नहीं, बल्कि मंदिरों का समूह है।
राजन	जी हाँ, यहाँ का मुख्य मंदिर लक्ष्मीनारायण का है जिस के गर्भ-गृह में विष्णु भगवान् के साथ लक्ष्मीजी की विशाल प्रतिमा स्थापित है। उस के दोनों ओर दुर्गा, हनुमान, शिवजी और अन्य देवी-देवताओं के मंदिर भी हैं।
पल्लवी	चलो, पहले लक्ष्मीनारायण के दर्शन लें। वहाँ मंदिर में आरती हो रही है।
आन्या	यह आपने कैसे पता लगाया, पल्लवी जी?
पल्लवी	आप घंटियों और कीर्तन की आवाज़ सुन रही हैं, न? यह भजन-कीर्तन आरती के समय होता है।
आन्या	अंत में पुजारी जो मिठाई बाँटते हैं, उसे क्या कहते हैं?
राजन	उसे प्रसाद कहते हैं और पवित्र मानते हैं।
आन्या	बहुत सुन्दर रस्म थी। आप लोग यहाँ अक्सर आते हैं?
पल्लवी	असल में रोज़मर्रा की भाग-दौड़ में यह रही जाता है। पर आना चाहिए।
राजन	सच। यह शांत वातावरण, फिर उस के बीच घंटियों की गूंज और धूप की सुगंध — मन को चैन मिलता है इस सब से।

8.3   Visiting a temple

The evening prayer service

Rajan	Anja, haven't you seen the Lakshminarayan temple yet?
Anja	No. Thank you for taking me with you.
Pallavi	This temple is packed to capacity on Diwali and Janamashtmi. Thank goodness it's still 12 days to Diwali!
Anja	I will be allowed to go in, won't I, even though I'm not a Hindu?
Pallavi	Oh yes, certainly. In our country, people of all faiths can enter every house of worship, whether it be a temple, a mosque or a church.
Anja	But I've seen certain temples in South India and Orissa that non-Hindus are not permitted to enter.
Rajan	What you're saying is right, however, there aren't many such temples. Look, here we are. Pallavi, do you want to offer some flowers?
Pallavi	Yes, let me just buy some. For you too, Anja?
Rajan	You need to leave your footwear here before going in.
Anja	Oh, what a big and peaceful place this is! It's not just one temple, it's a whole group of temples.
Rajan	Yes, the main temple here is the Laxminarayan temple, in the inner sanctum of which there is a large statue of Lord Vishnu together with the goddess Laxmi. And temples to Durga, Hanuman, Shiva and other deities are on both sides of it.
Pallavi	Let us first visit the Laxminarayan shrine. The prayer ceremony is being performed there.
Anja	How did you get to know that, Pallavi-ji?
Pallavi	Can you hear the sound of temple bells and hymns? This devotional singing accompanies the prayer ceremony.
Anja	And what's the sweet called that the priest distributes at the end?
Rajan	It's called *prasad* and it's considered to be sacred.
Anja	That was a very beautiful ceremony. Do you come here often?
Pallavi	Well, actually, we're so caught up in our daily routine that we don't get around to it. We ought to, though.
Rajan	True. This peaceful atmosphere, then the reverberation of the temple gong and the fragrance of incense … all this is very soothing for the mind.

शब्दावली   Glossary

8.1 दीपावली का पर्व: दीपों की रोशनी का त्योहार
8.1 Deepawali: the festival of lights

दीपावली/दीवाली *f* Diwali

पर्व *m* a festival

दीप/दीपक/दीया *m* a lamp, a light

रोशनी *f* light

त्योहार *m* a festival

ज़ोर-शोर *m* से with great enthusiasm

सफ़ाई *f* cleaning, tidying

तैयारी *f* preparation

बहाना *m* an excuse, a pretext

साफ़ clean

पुताई *f* whitewashing

संबंध *m* a connection

पुराना old, of long standing

प्रथा *f* a custom

लक्ष्मी/महालक्ष्मी *f* Lakshmi, the goddess of good fortune and wealth

पूजना to worship

सजाना to arrange, prepare, decorate

व्यापारी *m* a merchant, a trader

सजावट *f* arrangement, decoration

स्वच्छ clean, pure

स्थान *m* a place

प्रवेश *m* करना to enter

देवी *f* a goddess

धन-दौलत *f* wealth and riches

गणेश *m* Ganesh(a), the elephant-headed Hindu god of wisdom

सुख *m* happiness, joy

संपत्ति *f* wealth, riches, prosperity

सफ़लता *f* success

कामना *f* a wish, a desire

मूल original, basic, fundamental

कुटिया *f* a hut

चाहे... चाहे whether ... or

आलीशान magnificent

महल *m* a palace, a mansion

बत्ती *f* a light, a lamp

उज्जवलित lit up, aglow, ablaze

जलाना to light

महत्व *m* importance

मतलब *m* a meaning

मनाना to celebrate

कार्तिक/कार्त्तिक *m* the 8th month of the Hindu lunar year (October-November)

अमावस्या *f* the night of the new moon

पड़ना to occur, to take place

अंधेरी dark

अनगिनत innumerable, countless

जगमगाना to glitter, to sparkle

तमस् *f* darkness, ignorance

ज्योति *f* light, radiance

जीत *f* a victory

प्रतीक *m* a symbol

मानना to believe

रामचंदजी *m* the god Ram(a), hero of the epic poem *Ramayana*

वनवास *m* exile, banishment to a forest

विजयी victorious

अयोध्या *f* a North Indian town, in the epic poem *Ramayana* the birthplace of the god Rama

प्रांत *m* a region, a province, a state

अलग different

भाग *m* a part

उमंग *f* rapture, rejoicing, elation

रूप *m* a manner, a form

उत्सव *m* a festival

8.2 दीवाली मनाना: कुछ प्रथाएँ
8.2 Celebrating Diwali: some customs

पुणे *m* Pune, a city in the state of Maharashtra

कॉलेज *m* a college

स्कूल *m* a school

ख़ास तौर से *m* in particular, especially

रिवाज *m* a custom, a practice

मिट्टी *f* clay

मैदान *m* an open area, a playing field

मेला *m* a fair, a market held regularly at a fixed place

ख़ूबसूरत beautiful

हस्तशिल्प *m* handicraft

वस्तु *f* a thing, an article

बिकना to be sold

मोमबत्ती *f* a candle

पटाका *m* a firecracker

वग़ैरा/वग़ैरह and so forth, et cetera

रौनक़ *f* an atmosphere of excitement

ख़ासकर in particular, especially

बेचैनी *f* impatience, expectancy

इंतज़ार *m*/ इंतज़ारी *f* wait, expectation

बचपन *m* childhood

बेहद boundless, immense

अवसर *m* an occasion

ढेर-से lots of

पकवान *m* a delicacy, a treat

तरह-तरह (का/की/के) (of) many kinds, various

बाँटना to distribute, to share

भीड़ *f* a crowd, a crush

शुभकामना *f* a good wish

रंगोली *f* painted or floral decoration on a house wall or floor

इर्द-गिर्द all around

सूरज *m* the sun

डूबना to sink, to set (the sun)

नैवेद्य *m* an offering, food consecrated to a deity

चढ़ाना to offer to a deity

आतिशबाज़ी *f* fireworks

फुलझड़ी *f* a sparkler

अनार *m* Bengal light: a type of firework

शौक़ *m* interest, pleasure, eagerness

प्रदूषण *m* (environmental) pollution

लिहाज़ *m* consideration, deference

आस-पास round about, in the vicinity

सज्जा *f* decoration

मोहल्ला/मुहल्ला *m* a neighbourhood, a quarter (of a town)

टहलना to go for a walk, to stroll

उत्सुकता *f* eagerness, keenness

इंतज़ारी *f* / इंतज़ार *m* wait, expectation

8.3 मंदिर के दर्शन: संध्या की आरती
8.3 Visiting a temple: the evening prayer service

मंदिर *m* a temple

संध्या *f* the evening

आरती *f* a Hindu ceremony performed by moving a plate holding a lamp, incense, etc. in circles in front of a deity or person

लक्ष्मीनारायण *m* the depiction of the Hindu god Vishnu with his consort Lakshmi

जन्माष्टमी *f* a festival to celebrate the birth of the god Krishna

ख़चाख़च crowded, packed tightly

भरा full

शुक्र *m* gratitude

  शुक्र है कि... thankfully

बाक़ी remaining

धर्म *m* a religion

देव-स्थान *m* a place of worship

मस्जिद *m* a mosque

गिरजाघर /गिरजा *m* a church

दक्षिण south, southern

उड़ीसा *m* Orissa, a state in East India

ग़ैर-हिन्दु *m* a non-Hindu

मना होना prohibited, not permitted

जूता *m* a shoe

चप्पल *f* an open shoe, sandal

उतारना to take off (clothes/footwear)

शांत quiet, calm, peaceful

समूह *m* a collection, a group

मुख्य main, principal

गर्भ-गृह *m* the inner sanctum of a temple

विष्णु *m* Vishnu, one of the three main Hindu gods, seen as the preserver of the universe

भगवान् *m* a venerated deity, a god

विशाल huge

प्रतिमा *f* an image, a likeness, an idol

स्थापित placed, fixed

ओर *f* a side, a direction

दुर्गा *f* the goddess Durga

हनुमान *m* the chief of the monkeys in the epic *Ramayana*, worshipped by Hindus as a god

शिवजी *m* Shiv(a), one of the three main Hindu gods, seen as both the destroyer and the creator of the universe

देवता *m* a god

पता लगाना to find out

घंटी *f* a bell

कीर्तन *m* praising: group singing of hymns to a deity

आवाज़ *f* sound

भजन *m* a devotional song, a hymn

  भजन-कीर्तन *m* singing and praising

अंत *m* the end

पुजारी *m* the priest of a temple

प्रसाद *m* a devotional offering made to a god, typically food later shared among devotees

पवित्र pure, sacred

रस्म *f* a ceremony

अक्सर often

असल में in fact

रोज़मर्रा *m* daily, the daily life

भाग-दौड़ *f* hectic activity

वातावरण *m* atmosphere, environment

गूंज *f* reverberation, resonance

धूप *m* /धूपबत्ती *f* incense

सुगंध *f* fragrance, a sweet smell

मन *m* the mind

चैन *m* ease of mind, peace, repose

9
अवकाश और मन-बहलाव
Leisure and recreation

9.1 फ़िल्मों में दिलचस्पी

'बॉलीवुड' की चर्चा

अलका	सुनो, पल्लवी, कल सिनेमा देखने चलोगी? मुझे 'स्वदेस' के लिए दो टिकट मिले हैं और राहुल काम पर दिल्ली से बाहर गया हुआ है।
पल्लवी	'स्वदेस'? यह क्या बला है?
आन्या	आप को नहीं मालूम? यह शाह रुख़ ख़ान की नई पिक्चर है।
अलका	अरे वाह, तो आप हिन्दी फ़िल्मों में रुचि लेती हैं?
आन्या	जी हाँ, मुझे बॉलीवुड की फ़िल्मों का बेहद शौक़ है। और शाह रुख़ ख़ान का क्या कहना! फ़िल्मी जगत् के सितारों में मुझे वही सब से अच्छा लगता है।

अलका	तब तो फिर आप भी हमारे साथ चलिए, आन्या जी।पिक्चर यहीं नज़दीकी सिनेमा-घर में लगी है।
आन्या	धन्यवाद।अगर टिकट मिल जाए तो मैं भी चलूँगी।
पल्लवी	मेरी जान बख़्शो अलका, और मेरे बदले में इन्हें ही ले जाओ।आजकल की ऊल-जलूल फ़िल्मों के लिए मेरे पास फ़ालतू वक़्त नहीं है।
अलका	लेकिन यह आम बॉलीवुड हिट फ़िल्मों से अलग है, पल्लवी।
आन्या	जी हाँ, यह देश प्रेम के बारे मे है।
पल्लवी	अच्छा बताओ, इस फ़िल्म में गाने नहीं हैं?
अलका	गाने तो हैं, लेकिन ...
पल्लवी	कोई प्रेम कहानी भी होगी?
आन्या	जी हाँ, वह भी है।
पल्लवी	देखा न? वही मार-धाड़, वही पेड़ों के आगे-पीछे नाचते हुए हीरो-हीरोइन, वही ऊट-पटाँग कहानी जिस का सचाई से कोई लेना-देना ही न हो ... इस सब पर समय गँवाने का क्या फ़ायदा?
आन्या	तो आप को कैसी फ़िल्में पसंद हैं, पल्लवी जी?
अलका	इस मामले में तो पल्लवी बिलकुल कट्टर है।इस का केवल समांतर सिनेमा में मन लगता है।समाज और जीवन के गंभीर मुद्दों के बारे में सार्थक फ़िल्में, जिनमें न तो नाच हो, न संगीत, न ही प्रेम कथा।
पल्लवी	यही गंभीर सवाल ही हमारे समाज और हमारी ज़िंदगी की असलियत हैं।अफ़सोस की बात है कि ऐसी फ़िल्में कभी लोकप्रिय नहीं हो पातीं।
अलका	इसी लिए कि आम आदमी इन समस्याओं से वैसे ही हर समय घिरा रहता है।पैसा ख़र्च कर के वह सिनेमा-घर क्यों आता है? हक़ीक़त देखने के लिए नहीं, बल्कि अपना दिल बहला कर उसे भुलाने के लिए एक-आध घंटे के लिए ही सही।
पल्लवी	सपनों की दुनिया में भागने से समस्याएँ आप से आप हल तो होंगी नहीं।
अलका	तो तुम्हारा 'सार्थक' सिनेमा उपाय बताता है क्या? वह भी मनोरंजन का ही साधन है।जो बुद्धिजीवी दर्शक यह फ़िल्में देखते हैं, वे भी ख़याली पुलाव ही तो पकाते हैं।
पल्लवी	चलो, छोड़ो भी बहस — इस मामले में हमारे विचार हमेशा फ़र्क रहेंगे।

9.1   An interest in films

A discussion about 'Bollywood'

Alka	Listen, Pallavi, would you like to go to a movie tomorrow? I've got two tickets for 'Swades' and Rahul has gone out of Delhi on a business trip.
Pallavi	'Swades'? What on earth is that?
Anja	Don't you know? It's Shah Rukh Khan's new film.
Alka	Oh, great! You take an interest in Hindi films then?
Anja	Yes, I've a great passion for Bollywood films. And Shah Rukh Khan is out of this world! He's the star I like best in the film world.
Alka	Then do come with us too, Anja-ji. The film is showing at a cinema close to here.
Anja	Thank you. If I get a ticket, I'll come too.
Pallavi	Spare me the ordeal, Alka, and take her in my place. I have no time to spare for the silly films made these days.
Alka	But this is different from the usual Bollywood hits, Pallavi.
Anja	Yes, this is about patriotism.
Pallavi	All right, so tell me: are there no songs in this film?
Alka	There are songs, but…
Pallavi	There must be some sort of love story as well?
Anja	Yes, there is.
Pallavi	You see? Once more, mindless violence; yet again, the hero and heroine prancing around trees; yet again, a nonsensical plot that has nothing whatever to do with reality … what's the use of wasting time on all this?
Anja	So what kind of films do you like, Pallavi-ji?
Alka	Pallavi is completely fanatical in this matter. She's interested only in alternative cinema. Meaningful films about serious issues in society and life, in which there is no dance, no music, and no love story, either.
Pallavi	These serious questions are precisely the reality of our society and our lives. It's a pity that these films never manage to become popular.
Alka	That's because the common man is surrounded by these problems anyway. Why does he pay money and go to the cinema? Not to see reality, but to escape it by amusing himself, if only for a couple of hours.
Pallavi	Escaping to a world of fantasy won't get the problems sorted out on their own.

Alka   Well, does your 'meaningful' cinema offer any solutions? It's also just a means of entertainment. The intellectuals who watch these art house films are only building castles in the air as well.

Pallavi   Come, let's drop the argument – our views on this issue will always differ.

9.2   सांस्कृतिक गतिविधियाँ

संगीत और नृत्य का शौक़

अलका   आप भी फ़िल्म देखने चलेंगे, अजय जी? आन्या मेरे साथ जा रही है।

अजय   क्षमा कीजिएगा, मेरे पास आज काम बहुत है।

आन्या   इन्हें सिनेमा में वैसे भी कोई ख़ास दिलचस्पी नहीं है।

अलका   तो आप अवकाश में क्या करते हैं?

अजय   मैं संगीत से शग़ल करता हूँ।

अलका   तो आप संगीत के शौक़ीन हैं! किस तरह का संगीत पसंद है आपको?

अजय   हिंदुस्तानी शास्त्रीय संगीत मुझ को सबसे प्रिय है।

आन्या   इन के परिवार में सभी लोग संगीत प्रेमी हैं। कोई गाता है, तो कोई वाद्य बजाता है।

अलका   और आप, अजय जी?

अजय   पहले मुझे सितारवादन का बहुत शौक़ था, लेकिन अब रियाज़ के लिए इतना कम समय मिलता है कि मैं आजकल संगीत सुनने का ही आनंद लेता हूँ। कभी-कभी कुछ लिखता भी हूँ।

आन्या   संगीत के विषय पर अजय के लेख पत्रिकाओं में छपते रहते हैं।

अलका   और आप को भी भारतीय संगीत पसंद है, आन्या?

आन्या   जी हाँ, लेकिन मेरी ख़ास रुची भारतीय नृत्य में है।

अलका   वाह, बहुत ख़ूब! यहाँ तो आप दोनों को पूरे देश के जाने-माने कलाकारों को रंगमंच पर देखने का अवसर मिलेगा। दिल्ली में अक्तूबर से मार्च तक अनेक संगीत और नृत्य महोत्सव आयोजित किए जाते हैं।

अजय   आप ठीक कह रही हैं। दिल्ली की सांस्कृतिक संपदा का हम पूरा लाभ उठाएँगे। अगले महीने जो शंकरलाल संगीत समारोह होने वाला है उस में अपने प्रिय गायक पंडित जसराज को सुनने के लिए मैं आतुर हूँ।

आन्या	और मुझे कथक महोत्सव की इंतज़ारी है। किसी ज़माने में मुझे कथक सीखने की बहुत इच्छा थी लेकिन जर्मनी में इसका मौक़ा ही नहीं मिला।
अलका	तो अब आप दिल्ली में सीखिए न! मैक्स म्युलर भवन के पास ही कथक केंद्र है, जहाँ यह नाच सिखाया जाता है। आप को गुरु मिलने में कोई कठिनाई नहीं होनी चाहिए।
आन्या	सच? तब तो मैं वहाँ जा कर पता करूँगी। प्रोत्साहन देने के लिए धन्यवाद, अलका जी।
अलका	पल्लवी भी आप को कुछ जानकारी दे पाएगी। उस की बड़ी लड़की रेखा ने पढ़ाई के लिए पुणे जाने से पहले कई साल कथक केंद्र में नाच सीखा था। बहुत सुन्दर नाचती है वह।
आन्या	जी हाँ, मैं ज़रूर पता लगाऊँगी।
अजय	तुम्हें अपनी इच्छा पूरी करने का बढ़िया अवसर मिल रहा है, आन्या। इसे हाथ से जाने न देना!

9.2   Cultural activities

Music and dance as hobbies

Alka	Will you come with us to the film, too, Ajay-ji? Anja is going with me.
Ajay	I'm sorry, but I have a lot of work to do today.
Anja	He isn't particularly interested in films, anyway.
Alka	So what do you do in your free time?
Ajay	Music is my favourite pastime.
Alka	So you're a music aficionado! What kind of music do you like?
Ajay	I like Indian classical music best.
Anja	All his family members are music lovers. Some of them sing, others play an instrument.
Alka	And you, Ajay-ji?
Ajay	I used to be very fond of playing the sitar, but now I find so little time to practice that I savour the pleasure of just listening to music these days. Sometimes I write as well.
Anja	Ajay's articles on music keep appearing in print in periodicals.
Alka	And are you also fond of Indian classical music, Anja?
Anja	I am, but it is Indian dance that I have a special interest in.

Alka	That's wonderful! Both of you will have the opportunity of seeing renowned artistes from all over the country on stage here. Quite a few music and dance festivals are held in Delhi between October and March.
Ajay	You're right. We'll take full advantage of Delhi's cultural abundance. I can't wait to hear my favourite singer, Pandit Jasraj, perform in the Shankarlal Music Festival which takes place next month.
Anja	And I'm looking forward to the Kathak festival. There was a time when I really wanted to learn Kathak, but I just didn't get the chance to do so in Germany.
Alka	Well, learn it here then! The Kathak centre, where this dance form is taught, is quite close to Max Mueller Bhavan. You shouldn't have any difficulty in finding an instructor.
Anja	Really? Then I'll go there and find out. Thank you for the encouragement, Alka-ji.
Alka	Pallavi will also be able to give you some information. Her elder daughter, Rekha, learnt dance for many years at the Kathak centre before she went to Pune to study. She dances very beautifully.
Anja	Yes, I'll certainly find out.
Ajay	You're getting an excellent opportunity to fulfil your wish, Anja. Don't let it slip through your fingers!

9.3 खेल-कूद

किकेट के उन्माद में

अजय	राजन जी, हमें एक नए हैदराबादी खाने के रेस्तोराँ का पता चला है। वहाँ साथ चला जाए?
राजन	शौक़ से। हैदराबाद का खाना तो बहुत लज़ीज़ होता है।
अजय	आनेवाले शनिवार की शाम को आप को फ़ुरसत होगी?
राजन	आनेवाला शनिवार ... यानी सत्रह तारीख़? माफ़ कीजिए, लेकिन उस दिन तो बाहर निकलना असंभव होगा। शाम ही नहीं, मेरी सारी रात टीवी के सामने बीतेगी — देश के भविष्य का प्रश्न जो है।
आन्या	जी? मैं समझी नहीं। आजकल भारत में कहीं चुनाव तो नहीं हो रहे हैं।

अजय	यह बात सिर्फ़ क्रिकेट प्रेमी ही समझ पाएँगे। वह भी शायद सिर्फ़ भारत में क्योंक इतना लेकप्रिय यह खेल दुनिया में और कहीं नहीं है।
राजन	बात यह है, आन्या जी, कि आजकल वेस्टइंडीज़ में क्रिकेट विश्व कप प्रतियोगिता चल रही है और पूरे देश पर क्रिकेट का भूत सवार है। शनिवार की रात में भारत और बँगलादेश के बीच का मैच टीवी पर दिखाया जाएगा। विश्व कप के मैच देखने के लिए क्रिकेट के दीवाने रतजगा करने को भी तैयार होते हैं।
अजय	आप भी क्रिकेट के पीछे दीवाने है, राजन?
राजन	दीवानापन तो नहीं, दिलचस्पी कहूँगा। और आपको शायद दिलचस्पी भी नहीं है?
अजय	क्रिकेट से मेरा कभी भी ज़्यादा लगाव नहीं था, और जर्मनी में तो यह खेल अनजान के बराबर है।
आन्या	हमारे यहाँ फ़ुटबॉल सब से लोकप्रिय खेल है। जब जर्मनी में विश्व कप हुआ था, तब वहाँ भी चारों ओर फ़ुटबॉल का जोश फैला हुआ था।
राजन	अंतर बस यह है कि फ़ुटबॉल विश्व कप आप के देश में ही हुआ था, जबकि क्रिकेट विश्व कप भारत से हज़ारों मील दूर खेला जा रहा है।
अजय	अगर भारतीय टोली की पराजय हुई, तो इस उन्माद का क्या होगा?
राजन	उन्माद का यही तो ख़तरा है कि भावनाएँ काबू से बाहर हो जाती हैं। क्रिकेट-प्रेमी यह भूल जाते हैं कि हार-जीत हर खेल का हिस्सा है। अगर हमारी टीम हारी, तो वे खिलाड़ियों का बुरा हाल कर देंगे।

9.3   Sports and games

Cricket fever

Ajay	Rajan-ji, we've got to know of a new restaurant which serves Hyderabadi food. Should we go there together?
Rajan	With pleasure. Hyderabadi food is really delicious.
Ajay	Will you be free next Saturday?
Rajan	Next Saturday… that's the 17th, isn't it? I'm sorry, but it'll be impossible to go out on that day. Not just my evening but the whole night is going to be spent in front of the TV – after all, it's a question of the country's future.
Anja	I'm sorry? I don't quite follow. There isn't an election on anywhere in India these days, is there?

Ajay   This is something only cricket fans will understand. And that too perhaps only in India, because this game isn't nearly as popular anywhere else in the world.

Rajan   The thing is, Anja-ji, that the World Cup Championship is being played in the West Indies at present and the whole country is in the grip of cricket fever. The match between India and Bangladesh will be shown on TV on Saturday night. In order to see a World Cup match, cricket fans are ready even to stay up the whole night.

Ajay   Are you mad about cricket too, Rajan?

Rajan   I wouldn't call it madness; interest is more like it. And you're not even interested, it seems?

Ajay   I was never particularly fond of cricket, and in Germany the game is practically unknown.

Anja   Yes, the most popular game in our country is football. When the World Cup was held in Germany, there too football fever had taken hold everywhere.

Rajan   The only difference being that the football World Cup took place in your country, while the cricket World Cup is being played thousands of miles away from India.

Ajay   What will become of this frenzy if the Indian team loses?

Rajan   That's precisely the danger created by this kind of frenzy: that emotions spin out of control. Cricket fans forget that winning and losing are part of every game. If our team loses, they're going to make the players' lives miserable.

शब्दावली   Glossary

9.1 फ़िल्मों में दिलचस्पी: 'बॉलीवुड' की चर्चा
9.1 An interest in films: a discussion about 'Bollywood'

दिलचस्पी *f* an interest
चर्चा *f* a discussion, talk
सिनेमा *m* 1. cinema 2. film
बला *f* an awful/terrible person/thing
पिक्चर *f* a film
रुचि *f* an interest, a liking
बेहद boundless
शौक़ *m* interest, pleasure, eagerness
क्या कहना! *interjection* an expression of great admiration
जगत् *m* the world
सितारा *m* a star, a filmstar
नज़दीकी near, close
सिनेमा-घर *m* a cinema, a movie theatre
जान *f* life
बख़्शना to spare
बदले में in exchange, in place of
ऊल-जलूल silly, stupid, pointless
फ़ालतू surplus, spare
वक़्त *m* time
आम common, general
हिट *m/f* a hit, a popular film, song, etc.
अलग different
देश प्रेम *m* patriotism
गाना *m* a song, singing
प्रेम कहानी *f* a love story
मार-धाड़ *f* fighting, violence
पेड़ *m* a tree
आगे-पीछे front and back, around
नाचना dance
हीरो *m* a hero, a male lead (in a film)
हीरोइन *f* a heroine, a female lead (in a film)

ऊट-पटाँग nonsensical, absurd
कहानी *f* a story
सचाई *f* the truth
लेना-देना *m* a connection, a relationship
गँवाना to waste, to squander (as time, money, opportunity, etc.)
फ़ायदा *m* a benefit, an advantage
मामला *m* a matter
कट्टर fanatical, unyielding, strict
केवल only
समांतर parallel, alternative
मन लगना to like, to be pleased
समाज *m* society
जीवन *m* life, existence
गंभीर serious, thoughtful
मुद्दा *m* an issue, a matter
सार्थक *m* meaningful, significant
नाच *m* dance
संगीत *m* music
प्रेम कथा a love story
सवाल *m* a question, an issue, a problem
असलियत *f* the truth, a fact, reality
अफ़सोस *m* sorrow, regret
  अफ़सोस की बात a pity
लोकप्रिय popular
आम आदमी *m* the common man
घिरना to be surrounded
ख़र्च *m* expenses, outgoings
  ख़र्च करना to spend
हकीकत *f* reality
बल्कि but rather
भुलाना to erase from the mind, to forget

दिल बहलाना to distract, to divert the mind from cares
एक-आध one or two, a few
घंटा *m* an hour
सही / ही सही *interjection (at the end of a sentence)* at least
सपना *m* a dream
दुनिया *f* the world
भागना to run away, to flee, to avoid
समस्या *f* a problem
आप से आप of its own accord
हल *m* a solution (of a problem)

उपाय *m* a means, a measure, recourse
मनोरंजन *m* entertainment, amusement
साधन *m* a means
बुद्धिजीवी intellectual
दर्शक *m* a viewer
ख़याली पुलाव पकाना to build castles in the air
छोड़ना to let go, to give up
बहस *f* an argument/a dispute/a quarrel
विचार *m* an opinion, a thought, a viewpoint

9.2 सांस्कृतिक गतिविधियाँ: संगीत और नृत्य का शौक़
9.2 Cultural activities: music and dance as hobbies

संस्कृति *f* culture
सांस्कृतिक cultural
गतिविधि *f* an activity
संगीत *m* music
नृत्य *m* dance
क्षमा *f* pardon, forgiveness
अवकाश *m* / फ़ुरसत *m* leisure
शग़ल *m* a pastime, an occupation
(से) शग़ल करना to pass time, to occupy oneself (with)
शौक़ीन fond of, keen
शास्त्रीय संगीत *m* classical music
संगीत प्रेमी *m* a music lover
गाना to sing
वाद्य *m* a musical instrument
बजाना *an instrument* to play
सितारवादन *m* sitar playing
रियाज़ *m* practice
आनंद *m* enjoyment, delight
आनंद लेना to enjoy to the full
लेख *m* an article, an essay

पत्रिका *f* a magazine, a journal
छपना to be printed/published
ख़ूब fine, splendid
जाना-माना well known, renowned
कलाकार *m* an artist(-e), a performer
रंगमंच *m* a stage
समारोह *m* / महोत्सव *m* a festival
आयोजित करना organise
संपदा *f* an abundance
लाभ *m* a benefit, an advantage
लाभ उठाना to take advantage, to profit
गायक *m* a singer
आतुर impatient
कथक / कत्थक *m* a form of Indian classical dance
ज़माना *m* a time, a period
इच्छा *f* a wish
मौक़ा *m* a chance, an opportunity
केंद्र *m* a centre
गुरु *m* a teacher
इच्छा पूरी करना to fulfil a wish

कठिनाई *f*   a difficulty
प्रोत्साहन *m*   encouragement
नाचना   to dance

अवसर /मौका हाथ से जाने न देना   to not
       miss an opportunity/a chance

9.3 खेल-कूद: क्रिकेट के उन्माद में
9.3 Sports and games: cricket fever

खेल-कूद *m*   sport, games
उन्माद *m*   madness, frenzy, passion
शौक़ से   gladly, with pleasure
लज़ीज़   delicious, delightful
शनिवार *m*   Saturday
फ़ुरसत /फ़ुर्सत *f*   leisure, free time
तारीख़ *f*   a date
असंभव   impossible
बीतना   *time* to pass, to elapse
भविष्य *m*   the future
चुनाव *m/pl*   election(s)
क्रिकेट प्रेमी *m*   a cricket fan,
       a cricket lover
खेल *m*   a game
दुनिया *f*/विश्व *m*   the world
विश्वकप *m*   the world championship
प्रतियोगिता *f*   a competition
(किसी का)भूत सवार होना   to be
       obsessed (*by/with something*)
मैच *m*   a match
दीवाना   fanatical
रतजगा *m*   watching all night, vigil (on
       religious/festive occasions)
तैयार होना   to be ready
दीवानापन *m*   madness, a frenzy, mania
लगाव *m*   attachment, affection

अनजान   unknown
के बराबर   comparable to, equal
ओर *f*   a side, a direction
   चारों ओर   all around, everywhere, on
       all sides
जोश *m*   passion, enthusiasm
फैलना   to spread
अंतर *m*   a difference
हज़ार *m*   a thousand
मील *f*   a mile
टोली *f*/टीम *f*   a team
पराजय *f*/हार *f*   defeat
ख़तरा *m*   danger
भावना *f*   a feeling, an emotion
काबू *m*   control
भूलना   to forget
हार-जीत *f*   defeat and victory, losing
       and winning
जीत *f*   a victory, a win
हारना   to lose, to be defeated
हिस्सा *m*   a part
खिलाड़ी *m*   a player
(किसी का) बुरा हाल करना   to mistreat, to
       reduce (*someone*) to a
       sad state

10
पढ़ाई-लिखाई
Education

10.1 भारत में उच्च शिक्षा

अलग-अलग पाठ्यक्रम

अलका	राजन, क्या रेणु की वार्षिक परीक्षा के परिणाम आ गए?
राजन	नहीं, परीक्षा अभी चल रही है इसलिए पढ़ाई में जुटी हुई है बेचारी।
अजय	रेणु आपकी छोटी बेटी है, ना? वह पुणे विश्वविद्यालय में पढ़ रही है?
राजन	नहीं, वहाँ सिंबायोसिस नाम का एक संस्थान है जहाँ से वह एम.बी.ए. करने गई है।
अजय	सिंबायोसिस का तो बड़ा नाम है। लेकिन यह संस्थान काफ़ी नया है न?

अलका	जी हाँ, इसकी स्थापना किए गए तीस साल भी नहीं हुए लेकिन अब इसे देश के पाँच श्रेष्ठ प्रबंधन संस्थानों में से एक माना जाता है। बहुत कम समय में ही उसने अपना स्थान बना लिया।
अजय	मैंने सुना है कि इस पाठ्यक्रम में भरती होने के लिए जो प्रवेश-परीक्षा होती है, उस में सिर्फ़ कुछ ही गिने-चुने उम्मीदवार सफ़ल हो पाते हैं।
राजन	यह तो है। लेकिन आजकल तो हर जगह यही हाल है। शिक्षा और प्रशिक्षण के क्षेत्र में प्रतियोगिता बेहद बढ़ गई है।
अजय	हाँ, मैंने सुना है कि किसी-भी अच्छे संस्थान या विश्वविद्यालय में दाख़िला मिलना आसान नहीं होता।
अलका	सही है। ऐसा हमारे ज़माने में नहीं था। आजकल के बच्चों को पहले से कहीं ज़्यादा मेहनत करनी पड़ती है। पर रेणु ने इस इम्तहान की तैयारी में कोई कसर नहीं रखी थी और उसे अपनी मेहनत का फल मिल ही गया।
अजय	क्या आपकी बेटी ने बी.ए. भी पुणे से ही किया?
राजन	नहीं, स्नातक स्तर की शिक्षा उसने दिल्ली विश्वविद्यालय में ग्रहण की, मनोविज्ञान में। लेकिन अपनी बड़ी बहन के पूना जाने के बाद रेणु की भी वहीं पढ़ने की इच्छा थी। दोनों बहनों की आपस में बहुत बनती है।
अलका	दोनों लड़कियाँ बहुत होशियार हैं। बड़ी वाली, रेखा, तकनीकी मामलों में माहिर है।
अजय	अच्छा? क्या पढ़ा है उसने?
राजन	दिल्ली में सूचना प्रौद्योगिकी में स्नातकोत्तर स्तर प्राप्त किया। एम.टेक. की डिगरी लेने के बाद वह अभी पुणे में अनुसंधान कर रही है।
अजय	यह तो बड़ी अनोखी बात है कि उसने कम्प्यूटर विज्ञान जैसा विषय चुना। यह क्षेत्र परंपरागत तो लड़कियों का नहीं रहा है।
अलका	दुनिया बदल रही है, वह भी बड़ी तेज़ी से। आदमियों और औरतों के पेशों में बहुत जल्दी कोई अंतर नहीं रह जाएगा।

10.1   Higher education in India

A variety of courses

Alka	Rajan, have Renu's annual exam results come yet?
Rajan	No, the exam is still going on, so she is totally immersed in her studies, poor thing.

Ajay	Renu is your younger daughter, isn't she? Is she studying at Pune University?
Rajan	No, there's an institute called Symbiosis there where she's gone to do an MBA.
Ajay	Symbiosis has a very good reputation. But the institute is fairly new, isn't it?
Alka	Yes, it isn't quite 30 years since the institution was established, but it is now considered to be one of the five best management institutes in the country. It has made a place for itself in a very short time.
Ajay	I've heard that only a few selected candidates manage to pass the entrance test to get admission to this course.
Rajan	That's true. But these days it's the same everywhere. Competition has increased tremendously in the field of education and professional training.
Ajay	Yes, I've heard that getting admission to any good institute or university is not easy.
Alka	That's right. It wasn't like this in our time. Today's children have to work much harder than in the past. But Renu had spared no effort in preparing for this exam and in the end, she was rewarded for her labours.
Ajay	Did your daughter do her BA from Pune as well?
Rajan	No, she took a bachelor's degree in psychology from Delhi University. But after her elder sister left for Pune, Renu also wanted to study there. The two sisters get on very well.
Alka	Both girls are very bright. The older one, Rekha, is adept in technical matters.
Ajay	Really? And what did she study?
Rajan	She did her master's degree in information technology in Delhi. After taking an M. Tech degree, she's now doing research in Pune.
Ajay	It's unusual that she should have chosen a subject like computer technology. Traditionally this has hardly been a field for girls.
Alka	The world is changing, that too at a very rapid pace. Very soon there will be no difference between men's and women's professions.

10.2   जर्मनी में भारत-विद्या

भारत-विद्या क्यों?

पल्लवी	आन्या, आप ने हिन्दी हाइडलबर्ग विश्वविद्यालय में सीखी है, न?
आन्या	जी हाँ। मैंने वहीं एम.ए. किया है।
पल्लवी	और आप वहीं हिन्दी पढ़ाते थे, अजय जी?
अजय	जी हाँ।
पल्लवी	यानी जर्मनी में हिन्दी में एम.ए. किया जा सकता है?
आन्या	हिन्दी में नहीं, बल्कि भारत-विद्या में।
अजय	इस पाठ्यक्रम में हिन्दी भाषा के अलावा भारत से संबंधित अन्य विषय भी पढ़ाए जाते हैं।
पल्लवी	कौन-से विषय? साहित्य, राजनीति, वग़ैरह?
आन्या	हाँ, भारत का इतिहास, उस का धर्म और समाज, उस की कला और संस्कृति — यह सब पाठ्यचर्या का हिस्सा होते हैं।
पल्लवी	शिक्षा का माध्यम क्या होता है? हिन्दी?
आन्या	नहीं, नहीं, पढ़ाई ज़्यादातर जर्मन में ही होती है। और यह भी ज़रूरी नहीं है कि विद्यार्थी हिन्दी ही सीखें।
अजय	हाँ, पाठ्यक्रम में संस्कृत तो हमेशा शामिल होती है, लेकिन उस के सिवा कौन-कौन-सी भारतीय भाषाएँ सिखाई जाती हैं, यह तो हर विश्वविद्यालय के अपने संकाय पर निर्भर करता है।
पल्लवी	आपका मतलब है कि सिर्फ़ एक-दो ही नहीं, बल्कि कई जर्मन विश्वविद्यालयों में भारत-विद्या का पाठ्यक्रम चलाया जा रहा है?
अजय	बिल्कुल ऐसा ही है। और यही नहीं, यह प्रथा दो-ढाई सौ सालों से चली आ रही है।
पल्लवी	सच? यह तो अद्भुत बात है!
अजय	हमारे देश में लोग यह सुन कर अक्सर हैरान हो जाते हैं।
आन्या	यहाँ कई बार मुझ से लोगों ने पूछा है कि जर्मन नवयुवक किस मक़सद से हिन्दी पढ़ते हैं।
पल्लवी	यही सवाल मैं भी करने जा रही थी। क्योंकि रोज़गार मिलने में तो इस पढ़ाई का कोई ख़ास फ़ायदा होगा नहीं।
अजय	वैसे अध्ययन और अध्यापन किया जा सकता है। शोध-कार्य के बहुत-से क्षेत्र हैं ...

आन्या लेकिन कम ही लोग इस इरादे से भारत-विद्या की पढ़ाई शुरू करते
होंगे। कम से कम मेरे सहपाठियों में से कोई ऐसा नहीं था। इस विषय को
विद्यार्थी भारत में रुचि की वजह से चुनते हैं।

अजय हाँ, यह तो ठीक है। अधिकांश विद्यार्थियों का उद्देश्य यही होता है: भारत
के बारे में जिज्ञासा।

पल्लवी आपने यह पाठ्यक्रम क्यों चुना, आन्या?

आन्या जब मैं पंद्रह साल की थी तो मैंने अपने माँ-बाप के साथ भारत की यात्रा
की। उन तीन हफ़्तों में हम ने जो कुछ देखा, उस से मैं अत्यंत प्रभावित
हुई। मैंने तभी सोच लिया था कि मैं किसी न किसी तरह इस देश से संबंध
ज़रूर बनाऊँगी।

10.2   Indology in Germany

Why Indology?

Pallavi	Anja, you learnt Hindi at Heidelberg University, didn't you?
Anja	Yes. I did my MA there.
Pallavi	And is it there that you taught Hindi, Ajay-ji?
Ajay	That's right.
Pallavi	That means it's possible to do an MA in Hindi in Germany?
Anja	Not in Hindi, but in Indian Studies.
Ajay	Apart from Hindi, other subjects related to India are also taught in this course.
Pallavi	Which subjects? Literature, politics, and so on?
Anja	Yes, the history of India, its religion and society, its art and culture – all these are part of the syllabus.
Pallavi	What is the medium of instruction? Hindi?
Anja	No, no, the teaching is mostly in German. And it's not even necessary that the students learn Hindi.
Ajay	That's true. Sanskrit is always included in the curriculum, but apart from that, which Indian languages are taught depends on the faculty of each university.
Pallavi	You mean, a course in Indology is offered not just at one or two, but at many German universities?
Ajay	Exactly. And not only this, this tradition goes back two hundred or two hundred and fifty years.
Pallavi	Really? That's astonishing!
Ajay	In our country, people are often amazed when they hear this.

Anja	People here have often asked me for what purpose young people in Germany learn Hindi.
Pallavi	That's just the question I was going to ask. Because this course of study couldn't be of much use in finding employment.
Ajay	Well, one could go into teaching or research. There are many fields of research...
Anja	But there can't be many people who set out to study Indology with this aim in mind. Among my classmates, at least, there was nobody of this sort. Students opt for this subject because of an interest in India.
Ajay	Yes, that's right. The motive of most students is curiosity about India.
Pallavi	Why did you choose this subject, Anja?
Anja	When I was 15, I travelled to India with my parents. What we saw in those three weeks impressed me greatly. I decided right then that I would establish a connection with this country in one way or another.

शब्दावली   Glossary

10.1 भारत में उच्च शिक्षा: अलग-अलग पाठ्यकम
10.1 Higher education in India: a variety of courses

उच्च शिक्षा *f* higher education
वार्षिक annual
परीक्षा *f* an examination
परिणाम *m* result
जुटना to be involved/absorbed
एम.बी.ए. *m* an MBA
नाम होना to have a name/reputation,
        to be renowned
श्रेष्ठ best, most excellent
प्रबंधन संस्थान *m* a business school,
                a management institute
माना जाना to be considered
हालाँकि 1. although 2. however
स्थापना *f* establishment, founding
स्थान *m* a place, a position, a rank
पाठ्यकम *m* a course, a programme
भरती *f* admission, enrolment
प्रवेश-परीक्षा *f* an entrance examination
गिने-चुने selected
उम्मीदवार *m* a candidate, an applicant
सफ़ल successful
दाख़िला *m* admission
आसान easy
शिक्षा *f* education
प्रशिक्षण *m* training
प्रतियोगिता *f* competition
बेहद limitless, infinitely
बढ़ना to increase, to grow
ज़माना *m* a time, a period, the times
इम्तहान *m* an examination, a test
कसर *f* want, a shortcoming
 कसर *f* नहीं रखना/छोड़ना to leave
                nothing
                wanting

मेहनत *f* hard work, toil, industry
फल मिलना to obtain the fruits or
            results
स्नातक स्तर *m* a bachelor's degree
ग्रहण *m* acquisition, acceptance
 ग्रहण करना to accept, to obtain
बी.ए. *m* a bachelor's degree
मनोविज्ञान *m* psychology
आपस में among themselves, mutually
 आपस में बनना to get on with someone
होशियार intelligent
तकनीकी technical
मामला *m* a matter
माहिर *m* an expert
 (में) माहिर होना to be expert (in/at)
सूचना प्रौद्योगिकी *f* IT, information
                technology
स्नातकोत्तर postgraduate
स्तर *m* a level, a grade
प्राप्त करना to obtain
एम.टेक. *m* a master's degree in
            technology
डिगरी/डिग्री *f* a degree
अनुसंधान *m* research
अनोखा uncommon, unusual
कम्प्यूटर विज्ञान *m* computer science
परंपरागत traditional
दुनिया *f* the world
बदलना to change
तेज़ी *f* speed
पेशा *m* an occupation, a profession
अंतर *m* a difference

10.2: जर्मनी में भारत-विद्या: भारत-विद्या क्यों?
10.2 Indology in Germany: why indology?

भारत-विद्या *f* Indology, Indian studies
संबंधित connected
पाठ्यक्रम *m* a course, a programme
साहित्य *m* literature
राजनीति *f* politics
वगैरा/वगैरह and so on
इतिहास *m* history
धर्म *m* religion
समाज *m* society
कला *f* art
संस्कृति *f* culture
पाठ्यचर्या *m* a syllabus, course content,
      a curriculum
हिस्सा *m* a part
माध्यम *m* a medium
ज़्यादातर most, most commonly
विद्यार्थी *m, pl* a student
संस्कृत *f* the Sanskrit language
शामिल होना to be included
संकाय *m* a faculty
निर्भर dependent
प्रथा *f* a tradition, a custom

अद्भुत astonishing, remarkable
अक्सर often
हैरान amazed/perplexed
नवयुवक *m* youth
मक़सद *m* an aim, a purpose,
      an intention
रोज़गार *m* employment, work
फ़ायदा *m* an advantage, a benefit, gain
अध्ययन *m* study, research
अध्यापन *m* teaching
अध्ययन-अध्यापन *m* educational or
      academic work
शोध-कार्य *m* research work
इरादा *m* an intention, an aim, a goal
सहपाठी *m* a classmate
अधिकांश *m* 1. a majority
      2. on the whole
उद्देश्य *m* a purpose, a motive,
      an object
जिज्ञासा *f* desire to know, curiosity
अत्यंत extremely
प्रभावित influenced, impressed
संबंध *m* बनाना to establish a
      connection/link, to
      forge a relationship

11
काम-काज
Work and employment

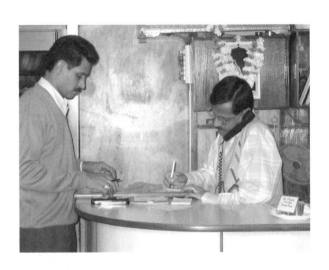

11.1 ड्राइवर रखना

नौकरी की शर्तें तय करना

राजकुमार   सलाम, साहब। आप को ड्राइवर की तलाश है? मेरा नाम राजकुमार है।

राजन   हाँ, आओ। तुम्हें किस ने भेजा है?

राजकुमार   तीसरी मंज़िल पर जो मल्होत्रा मैडम हैं, उनके ड्राइवर ने मुझे बताया।

राजन   तुम्हें गाड़ी चलाने का तजुर्बा है, राजकुमार?

राजकुमार   जी, साहब। सात साल से गाड़ी चला रहा हूँ।

राजन   अभी कोई नौकरी है तुम्हारे पास?

राजकुमार   जी, लेकिन सिर्फ़ महीने के अंत तक। जिन साहब के लिए मैं पिछले चार साल से काम कर रहा हूँ, उनका दिल्ली से बाहर तबादला हो गया है।

राजन	तुम कहाँ के रहनेवाले हो? दिल्ली के रास्ते-वास्ते सब पता हैं?
राजकुमार	हूँ तो गढ़वाल का लेकिन बचपन में ही दिल्ली आ गया था, इसलिए यहाँ की सब जगहों की जानकारी है।
राजन	यहाँ से कितनी दूर रहते हो? तुम्हारे बीवी-बच्चे भी हैं?
राजकुमार	जी, साहब। दो बेटे हैं, एक दस साल का, एक आठ साल का। मेरा घर पास में ही है, पटेल विहार में। साइकिल से बीस मिनट का रास्ता है।
राजन	यह तो बहुत अच्छी बात है। तो तुम यहाँ रोज़ सवेरे पौने आठ बजे हाज़िरी बजा सकोगे?
राजकुमार	जी। इस में कोई मुश्किल नहीं होगी।
राजन	इस नौकरी में समय की पाबंदी बहुत ही ज़रूरी है। मैं डाक्टर हूँ और अगर मैं मरीजों के पास देर से पहुँचूँ, तो सोचो उनका क्या हाल होगा!
राजकुमार	जी साहब, मैं समझा। मैं वक़्त का पाबंद ही हूँ। अभी तक किसी भी मालिक से इस बारे में शिकायत नहीं आई है।
राजन	आम तौर पर तुम्हारी ड्यूटी शाम को साढ़े छह बजे तक रहेगी, पर कभी-कभी देर भी हो सकती है। नियत समय के बाद काम करने के लिए पैसे तो मिलेंगें, लेकिन तुम देर तक रहने के लिए तैयार हो?
राजकुमार	कोई बात नहीं, साहब, यह तो ड्राइवर की नौकरी में होता ही है।
राजन	बहुत अच्छा। अब रही तनख़्वाह की बात। क्या माँग है तुम्हारी?
राजकुमार	यह तो आप ही बताइए, साहब। जो आप ठीक समझें।
राजन	आजकल ड्राइवरों का मासिक वेतन चार-पाँच हज़ार रुपये है, न?
राजकुमार	लेकिन साहब, वह रेट तो आठ घंटे के काम का है। आप की नैकरी में तो क़रीब-क़रीब ग्यारह घंटे की ड्यूटी है।
राजन	मुझे अपनी बात तो पूरी कर लेने दो, भलेमानस! काम के मुताबिक़ ही तनख़्वा मिलेगी। पहले महीने में तुम्हें साढ़े छह हज़ार मिलेंगे। तुम्हारा काम पसंद आने पर नौकरी एक महीने बाद सात हज़ार पर पक्की हो जाएगी। ओवरटाइम का तीस रुपये घंटा मिलेगा। दीवाली पर तुम्हें एक महीने की तनख़्वाह बोनस के तौर पर मिलेगी। मंजूर है?
राजकुमार	जी, साहब। और छुट्टी?
राजन	साल में तीन हफ़्ते छुट्टी ले सकते हो। हर इतवार को छुट्टी होगी और सब सरकारी छुट्टियों के दिनों पर भी। बस बिना बताए काम पर न आने के लिए तनख़्वाह कटेगी। अगर तुम यह सब शर्तें मानने को तैयार हो, तो अगले महीने की पहली तारीख़ से काम शुरू कर सकते हो।
राजकुमार	ठीक है, साहब। मैं पहली को पौने आठ बजे यहाँ पहुँच जाउँगा।

11.1   Employing a driver

Fixing the terms of employment

Rajkumar	Good afternoon, sir. You are looking for a driver, I believe? My name is Rajkumar.
Rajan	Yes, come in. Who has sent you?
Rajkumar	Mrs. Malhotra, who lives on the third floor – her driver told me.
Rajan	Do you have experience of driving a car, Rajkumar?
Rajkumar	Yes, sir. I've been driving for seven years now.
Rajan	Do you have a job at the moment?
Rajkumar	Yes, but only until the end of the month. The employer for whom I've been working for the past four years has been transferred out of Delhi.
Rajan	Where are you from? Do you know the routes and all in Delhi?
Rajkumar	I'm from Garhwal, actually, but I came to Delhi as a child, so I know my way around in the city.
Rajan	How far from here do you live? Are you married, any children?
Rajkumar	Yes, sir. I have two sons, one is ten, the other eight. My place is very close, in Patel Vihar. From here it takes ten minutes by bicycle.
Rajan	That's very good. So you'll be able to report for duty at eight in the morning every day?
Rajkumar	Yes, that won't be a problem.
Rajan	Punctuality is very important in this job. I'm a doctor, and if I reach my patients late, imagine what would happen to them!
Rajkumar	Yes sir, I understand. I'm always punctual. There have been no complaints about this so far from any of my bosses.
Rajan	You'll generally be on duty until 6.30 in the evening, but sometimes it can get later than that. You will of course be paid for working overtime, but are you ready to stay longer sometimes?
Rajkumar	That's all right, sir, it's part of a driver's job.
Rajan	Good. Now about your pay. What is your salary expectation?
Rajkumar	That's for you to say, sir. Whatever you think is right.
Rajan	The going rate for drivers these days is four to five thousand rupees per month, am I right?

Rajkumar	But sir, that's the pay for an 8-hour workday. With you, I'll be on duty for nearly 12 hours.
Rajan	Let me at least finish what I was saying, my good man! Of course you'll be paid according to your working hours. In the first month, you'll get six and a half thousand. If your work is satisfactory, your monthly salary will be fixed at 7000 rupees after the first month. Your overtime rate will be 30 rupees an hour. On Diwali, you will get one month's salary as an annual bonus. Agreed?
Rajkumar	Yes, sir. And what about leave?
Rajan	You can take three weeks' paid leave annually. You get Sunday off and all public holidays as well. However, pay will be deducted for being absent from work without prior notice. If you're ready to accept all these terms, you can start work on the first of next month.
Rajkumar	Right, sir. I'll be here at a quarter to eight on the first.

11.2   नौकरी से असंतुष्टी

32

पद त्यागने का निश्चय

पल्लवी	अरे अलका, तुम्हारी संस्था में जो शाख़ा प्रबंधक का पद ख़ाली था, उसका क्या हो रहा है? तुम ने इस पद के लिए आवेदन-पत्र भेजा था, न?
अलका	मैंने तुम्हें बताया था न कि मेरे अलावा दो और उम्मीदवार हैं? कल ही पता चला कि इस पद के लिए भारत भूषण को चुना गया है।
पल्लवी	क्या! तुम्हारा वह सहकर्मी जो सिर्फ़ अयोग्य ही नहीं, बल्कि कामचोर भी है? लेकिन इतना ऊँचा पद उस को मिला कैसे?
अलका	वह निर्देशक का चहेता जो ठहरा। इसी बात से तुम हमारे संस्थान की दुर्दशा का अनुमान लगा सकती हो। चापलूसी और चमचागिरी के बूते अब नालायक लोग तरक़्क़ी करने लगे हैं।
पल्लवी	यह तो बहुत अफ़सोस की बात है। तुम ने इस संस्थान में सात साल बहुत मन लगा कर काम किया है।
अलका	लेकिन मैंने तुम से कहा था न, कि नए निर्देशक ने सब कुछ चौपट कर दिया है। इस शख़्स के लिए ख़ाली आर्थिक लाभ माने रखता है। उसे हमारे सिद्धांतों की परवाह ही नहीं है।

पल्लवी	तो तुम्हारे और सहकर्ता भी असंतुष्ट हैं?
अलका	हाँ, कई लोग काम छोड़ने की सोच रहे हैं क्योंकि एक ओर कार्यभार बढ़ गया है और दूसरी ओर काम का वातावरण एकदम बिगड़ गया है। बहुत सोच-विचार के बाद अब मैंने भी इस्तीफ़ा देने का फ़ैसला कर लिया है।
पल्लवी	सच? लेकिन तुमने बहुराष्ट्रीय संस्था की पक्की नौकरी और मोटी आमदनी को त्याग देने के बारे में ठीक से सोच लिया है?
अलका	हाँ। इस तनाव के माहौल में मैं काम नहीं कर सकती। मैं इसी महीने अपना त्यागपत्र दे दूँगी।
पल्लवी	यह निर्णय तुम्हें बहुत समझ-बूझकर लेना चाहिए।
अलका	मैं जानती हूँ, लेकिन वैसे भी मैं बहुराष्ट्रीय संस्थाओं से ऊब चुकी हूँ। अब किसी स्वयं-सेवी संगठन में काम करना चाहती हूँ। आजकल कई ऐसी कल्याण-संस्थाएँ हैं जो अनेक क्षेत्रों में बहुत बढ़िया समाज सेवा कर रही हैं। उन्हें भी व्यावसायिक कार्यकर्ताओं की ख़ोज रहती है।
पल्लवी	तुम ठीक ही कहती हो। तुम्हारी प्रबंध और संपर्क के कार्य में इतनी योग्यता है कि तुम्हें आराम से अपनी पसंद की नौकरी मिल जाएगी।

11.2   Dissatisfaction with the job

The decision to resign

Pallavi	Listen, Alka, what's happening with the post of the branch manager which was vacant in your institute? You'd sent an application for the position, hadn't you?
Alka	I told you, didn't I, that there were two other candidates apart from me? I got to know just yesterday that Bharat Bhushan has been chosen for the post.
Pallavi	What! That colleague of yours who's not just incompetent but a shirker as well? But how did he manage to land such a high position?
Alka	He happens to be the director's blue-eyed boy, that's how. This matter gives you an idea of the plight of our institute. Unworthy people now get promoted on the strength of flattery and sycophancy.
Pallavi	That's a great pity. You've worked at this institute with such dedication for seven years.

Alka	But I'd told you, hadn't I, that this new director has ruined everything. Financial profit is the only thing that matters to this man. He doesn't give a fig about our principles.
Pallavi	So are your other colleagues also dissatisfied?
Alka	Yes. Many are thinking of leaving because on the one hand, the workload has increased, and on the other, the atmosphere at work has deteriorated dramatically. After mulling it over, now I've also decided to hand in my resignation.
Pallavi	Really? But have you thought it over seriously, giving up a permanent job and a fat salary in a multinational organization?
Alka	Yes, I have. I can't work in this tense environment. I'll hand in my letter of resignation this very month.
Pallavi	This is a decision you should consider very carefully.
Alka	I know, but I'm fed up of multinationals anyway. I'd like to work with an NGO now. These days there are many philanthropic organisations doing excellent social service in many fields. They're always on the lookout for qualified professionals, too.
Pallavi	You're right. With your qualifications in management and in liaison work, you'll easily find the job of your choice.

11.3   नई नौकरी

ग़ैर-सरकारी संगठन का काम

राजन	नई नौकरी के लिए बधाई हो, अलका! पल्लवी ने बताया कि आप अपने नए काम से बहुत ख़ुश हैं।
अलका	जी हाँ। समाज के लिए जो काम मुझे 'बापू शांति प्रतिष्ठान' में करने का अवसर मिल रहा है, वैसा ही काम करने की मुझे बहुत दिनों से इच्छा थी।
राजन	बहुत आदर्शवादी विचार हैं आपके। जो आप की पहले वाली नौकरी थी, उसे छोड़ने को कम ही लोग तैयार होते।
अलका	डाक्टर होने के नाते आप तो जानते ही हैं कि सिर्फ़ धन कमाने के लिए काम करने से मन को तृप्ति नहीं मिलती। वैसे समाज सेवा करने वाले ग़ैर-सरकारी संगठनों की स्तिथि अब पहले से काफ़ी सुधर गई

है। आजकल इस क्षेत्र में भी योग्य लोगों की कमाई उतनी ही होती है जितनी अन्य क्षेत्रों में।

पल्लवी	अलका, कुछ मिठाई-विठाई तो ख़िलाओ! काम शुरू किए अभी दो महीने भी नहीं हुए और इसी बीच में तुम्हारी तरक़्क़ी भी हो गई।
राजन	अरे वाह! इतनी कम अवधि में आप इतनी कामयाब हो पाईं, इसके लिए भी बधाई।
अलका	धन्यवाद। लेकिन यह कोई बहुत बड़ी उपलब्धि नहीं है। साक्षरता अभियान का संचालन मुझे सौंप दिया गया है क्योंकि हम लोगों का काम बहुत बढ़ गया है और प्रतिष्ठान में फ़िलहाल लोगों की कमी है।
राजन	और आप ने किस पद पर काम शुरू किया था?
अलका	तब मुझे संपर्क अधिकारी के पद पर लिया गया था।
राजन	बापू शांति प्रतिष्ठान साक्षरता के सिवा और क्षेत्रों में भी सक्रिय है, न? मुझे याद है कि मेरे हस्पताल ने एक बार आप की संस्था के साथ ग्रामीण स्वास्थ्य पर एक कार्यशाला का आयोजन किया था।
अलका	जी हाँ, हमारी स्वास्थ्य, कुटीर उद्योग और प्रौढ़ शिक्षा से संबंधित परियोजनाएँ भी हैं। अनेक छोटे स्वयं-सेवी संगठन हैं जो वंचित वर्ग के लोगों के रहन-सहन में सुधार लाने की कोशिश में लगे हैं। हम लोग इन संगठनों के कार्यक्रमों को सहयोग देते हैं।
राजन	इतना नेक काम करने वाले सभी लोगों को हमें दाद देनी चाहिए!

11.3 A new job

Working for a non-governmental organisation

Rajan	Congratulations on the new job, Alka! Pallavi told me that you're very happy with your new work.
Alka	I am indeed. The social work that I'm getting the chance to do at the Bapu Peace Foundation is just the kind of work I've wished to do for a long time.
Rajan	Your views are very idealistic. Few people would have been ready to leave the job you had before.
Alka	As a doctor, you'd know that working just for the sake of earning money doesn't bring mental satisfaction. And besides, the state of the NGOs involved in social work has improved considerably compared to the past. Nowadays qualified people earn as much in this field as in others.

Pallavi	You should be treating us to sweets, Alaka! It hasn't even been two months since you started work, and you've already got a promotion in the meanwhile.
Rajan	That's fantastic! Congratulations again for making your mark in such a short period.
Alka	Thank you. But it's no great achievement. I was entrusted with running the literacy campaign because our work has increased a lot and there's a shortage of staff in the foundation.
Rajan	And in what position did you start work?
Alka	I was appointed to the post of liason officer.
Rajan	Apart from literacy, the Bapu Peace Foundation is active in other fields, too, isn't it? I remember that my hospital once organised a workshop on rural health together with your institution.
Alka	Yes, we have projects related to health, cottage industry and adult education too. There are a number of small voluntary organisations trying to improve the living conditions of the deprived section of the population. We cooperate in the programmes of these organisations.
Rajan	I take my hat off to everyone who does such worthy work!

शब्दावली   Glossary

11.1 ड्राइवर रखना: नौकरी की शर्तें तय करना
11.1 Employing a driver: fixing the terms of employment

शर्त *f* a condition, terms
तलाश *f* search
भेजना to send
मंज़िल *f* a storey, a floor
गाड़ी चलाना to drive a car
तजुर्बा/तजुरबा/तजरबा *m* experience
तबादला *m* a transfer
गढ़वाल *m* Garhwal, a mountainous region in North India
जानकारी *f* knowledge, information
बचपन *m* childhood
बीवी *f* a wife
साइकिल *f* a bicycle
हाज़िरी *f* बजाना to report on duty
मुश्किल *f* difficulty
पाबंदी *f* due observance
वक़्त/समय की पाबंदी *f* punctuality
समय *m*/वक़्त *m* time

ड्यूटी *f* duty, work
नियत fixed, appointed, arranged
तनख़्वाह *f*/तनख़्वा *f*/वेतन *m* salary, pay
माँग *f* demand
मासिक monthly
रेट *m* a rate, a standard payment
करीब-करीब almost
भलामानस *m* a good man, a courteous person; *ironic* simpleton
(के) मुताबिक़ according (to)
पक्की fixed, definite, determined
ओवरटाइम *m* overtime
बोनस *m* a bonus
तौर *m* a way, a manner
के तौर पर by way of
मंज़ूर accepted, agreeable, approved of
मानना to agree
तारीख़ *f* a date

11.2 नौकरी से असंतुष्टी: पद त्यागने का निश्चय
11.2 Dissatisfaction with the job: the decision to resign

असंतुष्टि *f* dissatisfaction
त्याग-पत्र *m* a letter of resignation
निश्चय *m* a decision, a resolve
संस्थान *m*/संस्था *f* institute, organisation
शाख़ा *f* a branch
प्रबंधक *m* a manager
पद *m* a post, a position
आवेदन-पत्र *m* an application

उम्मीदवार *m* an applicant, a candidate
चुनना to choose, to select
सहकर्मी *m* a colleague
अयोग्य incapable, incompetent
कामचोर *m*, *adj.* idle, an idler, a shirker
निर्देशक *m* a director
चहेता *m* dear one, darling, a favourite
दुर्दशा *f* sad plight, misery

अनुमान *m*   a guess, a conjecture,
          an estimate
अनुमान लगाना   to suppose, to estimate
चापलूसी *f*   flattery, sycophancy
चमचागिरी *f*   flattery
बूता *m*   power, strength, might
  के बूते पर   on the strength of
नालायक   incapable, unworthy
तरक़्क़ी *f*   a promotion, progress
  तरक़्क़ी करना   to make progress, to do
               well, to develop
चौपट *f*   a waste, a ruin
  चौपट करना   to ruin, to corrupt
शख़्स *m*   a person, an individual
ख़ाली   only
आर्थिक   monetary, financial
लाभ *m*   a profit, an advantage
माने *m*   meaning
सिद्धांत *m*   a principle
परवाह / परवा *f*   care, concern
  (की) परवाह करना   to care (about)
सहकर्ता *m*   a colleague
असंतुष्ट   dissatisfied, displeased
छोड़ना   to leave, to give up, to resign
  काम छोड़ना   to resign a post
कार्यभार *m*   workload
वातावरण *m*   an environment, a mood,
            an atmosphere

बिगड़ना   to deteriorate, to be spoiled
सोच-विचार *m*   reflection, consideration
फ़ैसला *m* /निर्णय *m* /निश्चय *m*   a decision
इस्तीफ़ा *m*   a resignation
  इस्तीफ़ा देना   to resign
बहुराष्ट्रीय   multinational
आमदनी *f*   an income
त्यागना   to give up
तनाव *m*   tension
माहौल *m*   an environment, a mood,
            an atmosphere
निर्णय *m*   a decision, a conclusion
  निर्णय लेना /करना   to decide
समझ-बूझकर   with due caution,
                prudently
ऊबना   to be dispirited, to be bored
स्वयं सेवी   a volunteer
संगठन *m*   an organisation
कल्याण-संस्था *f*   a welfare organisation
क्षेत्र *m*   an area, a sphere of action
समाज सेवा *f*   social work, social service
व्यावसायिक   professional, occupational
कार्यकर्ता   a worker
प्रबंध *m*   organisation, management
संपर्क *m*   contact, liaison, a relationship
योग्यता *f*   qualification(s), ability
आराम से   with ease

11.3 नई नौकरी: ग़ैर-सरकारी संगठन का काम
11.3 A new job: working for a non-governmental organisation

ग़ैर-सरकारी   non-governmental
ग़ैर-सरकारी संगठन *m*   an NGO, a non-
            governmental organisation
बधाई *f*   congratulation(s)
बापू *m*   a father, *'Father of the nation'*,
        title used for M.K. Gandhi

के नाते   because of
शांति *f*   peace, tranquillity
प्रतिष्ठान *m*   a foundation, an nstitute
इच्छा *f*   a wish
आदर्शवादी   idealistic

विचार *m* a thought, an idea, a view
धन *m* money, riches, wealth
कमाना to earn
तृप्ति *f* satisfaction
स्तिथि *f* circumstances, situation, state
सुधरना to improve
कमाई *f* earnings
योग्य qualified, capable
तरक़्क़ी *f* a promotion, progress
अवधि *f* a set time, a period
कामयाब successful
उपलब्धि *f* an achievement
साक्षरता *f* literacy
अभियान *m* a campaign
संचालन *m* management
सौंपना to entrust, to hand over
फ़िलहाल at the present time
कमी *f* a deficit, a shortage

संपर्क अधिकारी *m* a PR Manager, a liaison officer
सक्रिय active
ग्रामीण rural
कार्यशाला *f* a workshop
आयोजन *m* organisation, arrangement
कुटीर उद्योग *m* a cottage industry
प्रौढ़ शिक्षा *f* adult education
संबंधित connected
परियोजना *f* a project
वंचित deprived
वर्ग *m* a social group, a class
रहन-सहन *m* a lifestyle
सुधार *m* an improvement
कोशिश *f* an effort, an attempt
सहयोग *m* support, cooperation
नेक good, excellent, worthy
दाद *f* praise, appreciation

12
राजनीति
Politics

12.1   उत्तर प्रदेश में विधानसभा चुनाव

चुनावी नतीजे

अलका	पल्लवी, तुम ने आज का अख़बार देखा है?
पल्लवी	अरे नहीं, आज सवेरे हमारा अख़बार ही नदारद था। पता नहीं कमबख़्त अख़बारवाले को क्या हो गया। यूपी के चुनाव की क्या ख़बर है?
अलका	सनसनीख़ेज़ ख़बर है। दैनिक 'जनसत्ता' ने सुर्ख़ी लगाई है: उत्तर प्रदेश में तूफ़ान, बसपा की गाज।
पल्लवी	अरे वाह, तो मायावती की बहुजन समाज पार्टी जीत गई! बहुत अच्छा हुआ। कल टीवी पर जो शुरू के आँकड़े दिखाए थे उन का रुझान भी इसी तरफ़ था।

अलका	कल रात तक मतों की गिनती जारी थी लेकिन अब नतीजे की घोषणा कर दी गई है। अब मायावती को मुख्यमंत्री पद की शपथ लेने के लिए बुलाया जाएगा।
पल्लवी	तो बहुजन समाज पार्टी राज्य सरकार बनाने के लिए कौन-से दल के साथ गठजोड़ करेगी?
अलका	यही तो चमत्कारी बात है। बसपा ने पूर्ण बहुमत हासिल कर ली है इस लिए सत्ता अकेले उसी के हाथ में है।
पल्लवी	यानी बसपा अकेले अपने दम पर सरकार बनाने की स्तिथि में पहुँच गई! यह तो किसी ने सोचा भी नहीं था। इस के माने कि मायावती का समर्थन सिर्फ़ दलितों और मुसलमानों ने नहीं किया, हालाँकि वे दलितों के अधिकारों के लिए लड़ती रही हैं।
अलका	हाँ, उन्हें सभी धर्मों और जातियों के लोगों के वोट मिले हैं। यह जीत सचमुच ऐतिहासिक है। सभी समाचार पत्र मायावती की रणनीति की तारीफ़ कर रहे हैं।
पल्लवी	इस मतदान से यह साबित होता ही कि हमारे देश की आम जनता का लोकतंत्र में अटूट विश्वास है।
अलका	शायद यह परिणाम देश की राजनीति को भी एक नई दिशा दे।

12.1   State assembly elections in Uttar Pradesh

The election results

Alka	Pallavi, have you seen today's newspaper?
Pallavi	No, I haven't, our paper was missing this morning. God knows what happened to the wretched paperboy. What news of the election in UP?
Alka	The news is sensational. The daily, Jansatta, carried the headline: 'Storm in Uttar Pradesh, thundering victory for BSP'.
Pallavi	Wow, Mayavati's Bahujan Samaj Party has won then! That's very good. The preliminary statistics they showed on TV yesterday also showed a tendency in this direction.
Alka	Vote counting was in progress until last night, but the results have been declared now. Mayavati will now be called to take the oath of office as Chief Minister.
Pallavi	So which party will the Bahujan Samaj Party coalesce with to form the state government?

Alka	That's just the remarkable thing. BSP has won an absolute majority, so the electoral mandate is solely in its hands.
Pallavi	That means the BSP has reached a position in which it can form a government on its mettle alone! Nobody had even thought that this could happen. This means it wasn't just the Dalits and Muslims who supported Mayavati, though she's been fighting for Dalit rights all along.
Alka	Yes, she won the votes of people belonging to all religions and castes. This is a truly historic victory. All the newspapers are praising her electoral campaign strategy.
Pallavi	This election goes to prove that the common people in our country have unshakeable faith in democracy.
Alka	This result might even lead the country's politics in a new direction.

12 .2   आतंकवादी हमला

34

ट्रेनों में विस्फोट

आन्या	आपने मुंबई के विस्फोटों की ख़बर सुनी?
अलका	हाँ, मैंने अभी-अभी दूरदर्शन पर समाचार देखे। कितना भयानक हादसा हो गया!
पल्लवी	क्यों, क्या हुआ बंबई में?
अलका	अरे, तुम ने नहीं सुना? शहर की लोकल ट्रेनों पर आतंकवादियों ने हमला किया।
पल्लवी	कब हुआ यह?
आन्या	आज शाम को छह बजे के क़रीब, सब से ज़्यादा भीड़वाले समय पर, जब लोग अपने दफ़्तरों से घर लौट रहे होते हैं।
पल्लवी	हाय राम! उस समय तो बंबई की ट्रेनों में पैर रखने की जगह नहीं रहती।
अलका	हमलावारों का यही उद्देश्य था कि ज़्यादा से ज़्यादा लोगों की हत्या हो। कुछ ही मिनटों के अंदर आधा दर्जन ट्रेनों में एक के बाद एक सात बम धमाके हुए।
आन्या	ख़बरों के अनुसार इन सिलसिलेवार धमाकों में दो सौ लोग मारे गए और सात सौ से अधिक घायल हुए।

पल्लवी	कुछ मालूम हुआ है कि हत्यारे कौन हैं? क्या यह आत्मघाती हमले थे?
आन्या	अभी तक वारदात की ज़िम्मेदारी किसी चरमपंथी गुट ने नहीं ली है। हालाँकि शक उन्हीं पर है।
अलका	केंद्रीय गृहमंत्री ने कहा है कि कुछ सुराग़ मिले हैं और जांच पूरी तेज़ी से चल रही है। लेकिन हमले के पीछे किस का हाथ है, यह अभी कहा नहीं जा सकता।
आन्या	मुंबई पुलिस ने भरोसा दिलाया है कि वह जल्दी ही अभियुक्तों को पकड़ लेगी। शहर की सुरक्षा व्यवस्था काफ़ी कड़ी कर दी गई है।
पल्लवी	इस ख़ौफ़नाक घटना ने तो मुंबई को झकझोर के रख दिया होगा।
अलका	मुंबई क्या, पूरा देश ही हिल गया है। विस्फोटों के थोड़ी ही देर बाद प्रधान मंत्री ने दूरदर्शन और रेडियो पर राष्ट्र को संबोधित किया था।
पल्लवी	क्या कहा उन्होंने?
आन्या	यही कि सरकार अपने बल-बूते से कट्टरपंथी के ख़िलाफ़ लड़ रही है लेकिन हर नागरिक को भी चौकसी बरतनी पड़ेगी।
अलका	देश में आतंकवाद से ख़तरा वाकई बहुत बढ़ गया है। हाल ही में दिल्ली, बनारस और बैंगलोर में जो विस्फोट हुए थे, वे भी भारी भीड़ वाली जगहों में हुए। यह आम लोगों में डर पैदा करना के तरीके हैं।
पल्लवी	हाँ, ऐसे हालात में बिना सहमे हुए सतर्क रहने की ज़रूरत है।

12.2   A terrorist attack

Bomb explosions on trains

Anja	Did you hear the news about the explosions in Bombay?
Alka	Yes, I just saw the news on televison. What a terrible thing to happen!
Pallavi	Why, what happened in Bombay?
Alka	What, haven't you heard? Terrorists attacked the city's local trains.
Pallavi	When did this happen?
Anja	This evening at about six, during rush hour, when people were returning home from their offices.
Pallavi	Oh God! The commuter trains in Bombay are jam-packed at that time!

Alka	That was precisely the attackers' intention, to kill as many people as possible. Within the space of a few minutes, there were seven bomb blasts, one after the other, on six trains.
Anja	According to the news reports, 200 people have been killed and over 700 injured in this series of blasts.
Pallavi	Has anything come to light about who the bombers were? Were these suicide attacks?
Anja	None of the extremist groups has claimed responsibility for the incident so far. It is on them that suspicion has fallen, though.
Alka	The union Home Minister said that some clues have been found and a full-scale investigation is being conducted. But it is too early to say who was behind the attack.
Anja	The police in Bombay have assured people that they will find the culprits very soon. Security measures in the city have been tightened considerably.
Pallavi	This terrifying incident must have devastated Mumbai.
Alka	Not just Bombay, the whole country is shaken. Shortly after the explosions, the Prime Minister addressed the nation on TV and radio.
Pallavi	What did he say?
Anja	Just that the government is fighting with all its might against the extremists, but every citizen will also have to be vigilant.
Alka	The danger of terrorism has indeed intensified in the country. The bomb blasts that went off in Delhi, Benares and Bangalore recently were also in crowded places. These are tactics to create fear among ordinary people.
Pallavi	Yes, in these circumstances it is necessary to stay alert without being scared.

शब्दावली   Glossary

12.1 उत्तर प्रदेश में विधानसभा चुनाव: चुनावी नतीजे
12.1 State assembly elections in Uttar Pradesh: the election results

उत्तर प्रदेश/यूपी/उ.प्र. *m* Uttar Pradesh, a state in North India

विधानसभा *f* the Legislative Assembly

चुनाव *m* an election

चुनावी नतीजा *m* an election result

अख़बार *m* a newspaper

नदारद absent/gone, lost

कमबख़्त wretched

अख़बारवाला *m* a paperboy

ख़बर *f* the news

सनसनीख़ेज़ sensational

दैनिक daily

जनसत्ता *f* a Hindi daily newspaper

सुर्ख़ी *f* a headline

तूफ़ान *m* a storm

गाज *m* a thunderbolt, lightning

बहुजन समाज पार्टी/बसपा *f* a national political party formed chiefly to represent Dalits

जीतना to win

आँकड़ा *m* an estimate, figure, statistics

रुझान *m* a tendency, an inclination

मत *m* a vote

गिनती *f* counting

जारी progressing, continuing

घोषणा *f* an announcement

मुख्यमंत्री *m* chief minister

शपथ *f* oath

 शपथ लेना to take an oath

बुलाना to call, to summon, to send for

राज्य सरकार *f* the state government

दल *m* a (political) party, a group

अटूट unfailing, inexhaustible

विश्वास *m* faith, belief

गठजोड़/गँठजोड़ *m* an alliance

चमत्कारी astonishing, wonderful

पूर्ण whole, full

बहुमत *f* a majority

पूर्ण बहुमत *f* an absolute majority

हासिल करना to acquire, to get

सत्ता *m* power, authority (political or administrative)

दम *m* strength, vigour, mettle

स्थिति *f* 1. a position 2. a situation

समर्थन *m* support

दलित trampled, oppressed

दलित *m* Dalit. Self-designation for a group of people traditionally regarded as low-caste or untouchables

मुसलमान *m* a Muslim

राजनीति *f* politics

नेता *m* a leader, a politician

धर्म *m* a religion

जाति *f* a caste

वोट *m* a vote

जीत *f* a victory, a win

ऐतिहासिक historic

समाचार पत्र *m* a newspaper

रणनीति *f* a campaign strategy

तारीफ़ *f* praise

मतदान *m* voting, to vote

साबित proved, confirmed

जनता *f* the people, the populace

आम जनता *f* the common people

लोकतंत्र *m* democracy

परिणाम *m* a result

दिशा *f* a direction

12.2 आतंकवादी हमला: ट्रेनों में विस्फोट
12.2 A terrorist attack: bomb explosions on trains

आतंकवादी *m*   a terrorist
हमला *m*   an attack
विस्फोट *m*   an explosion
दूरदर्शन *m*   the television
समाचार *m*   the news
भयानक   terrible
हादसा *m*   an incident, an accident
लोकल ट्रेन *f*   a local/commuter train
भीड़ *f*   a crowd
दफ़्तर *m*   an office
हाय राम! *interjection* oh God!
पैर रखने की जगह न होना   to be jam-
                                   packed
हमलावार *m*   an attacker
उद्देश्य *m*   an intention, a purpose,
                        an object
हत्या *m*   a killing, a murder
बम *m*   a bomb
धमाका *m*   a loud noise, blast, explosion
सिलसिलेवार   linked, serial, sequential
मारे जाना   to be killed
घायल   wounded, injured
हत्यारा *m*   a murderer
आत्मघात *m*   a suicide
वारदात *f*   an event, an incident,
                     a disaster
ज़िम्मेदारी *f*   responsibility
चरमपंथी *m*   an extremist
गुट *m*   a group, a faction
शक *m*   a suspicion
केंद्रीय   central
गृहमंत्री *m*   the home minister
सुराग *m*   a sign, a trace, a clue

जाँच *f*   an investigation, an enquiry
तेज़ी *f*   speed
भरोसा *m*   confidence, faith, hope
  भरोसा दिलाना   to assure
अभियुक्त *m*   a culprit, the accused
सुरक्षा *f*   security, safety
व्यवस्था *f*   an arrangement,
                      a step, measures
कड़ा   tight, tough
ख़ौफ़नाक   fearsome, terrifying
घटना *f*   a happening, an incident,
                  an event
झकझोर देना   to shake violently, to jolt
हिल जाना   to be shaken, agitated
प्रधान मंत्री *m*   the prime minister
राष्ट्र *m*   a nation, a country
संबोधित करना   to address
बल-बूता *m*   power, strength, might
कट्टरपंथी *m*   a fanatic
के ख़िलाफ़   against
लड़ना   to fight
नागरिक *m*   a citizen
चौकसी *f* बरतना   to be alert/vigilant
आतंकवाद *m*   terrorism
ख़तरा *m*   danger
हाल में   recently
भारी   1. heavy 2. vast, crowded
डर *m*   fear
पैदा करना   to create, to produce
तरीक़ा *m*   a method, a way, a tactic
हालात *f*   a particular state,
                 circumstances
सहमना   to feel fear
सतर्क   alert, watchful

13
टेलीफ़ोन पर बातें
Phone calls

13.1   ग़लत नंबर मिलना

 35

बदला हुआ टेलीफ़ोन नंबर

आवाज़	हेलो।
आन्या	नमस्ते। मेरा नाम आन्या कुमार है। मैं आप के केंद्र में कथक शिक्षण के बारे में जानकारी चाहती …।
आवाज़	हेलो, मैडम, आप ने कौन-सा नंबर मिलाया है?
आन्या	आप कथक केंद्र से नहीं बोल रहे हैं?
आवाज़	नहीं जी। आप को ग़लत नंबर मिल गया है।
आन्या	ओ, माफ़ कीजिएगा।
आवाज़	कोई बात नहीं।

आन्या	(फिर से नंबर मिलाती है)
आवाज़	हेलो।
आन्या	ओह! क्षमा कीजिए, फिर से ग़लत नंबर मिल गया है।
आवाज़	मैडम, कौन-सा नंबर मिला रही हैं आप?
आन्या	दो तीन तीन सात चार छह दो शून्य।
आवाज़	नंबर तो यही है, लेकिन यहाँ कोई केंद्र-वेंद्र नहीं है। यह मेरे घर का नंबर है। नंबर पहले चेक कीजिए, न। आप तो बार-बार यहीं फ़ोन करतीं हैं।

13.1   Dialing the wrong number

A changed telephone number

Voice	Hello.
Anja	Good morning. My name is Anja Kumar. I would like some information about Kathak classes at your centre ...
Voice	Hello, Madam, what number have you dialled?
Anja	Aren't you speaking from the Kathak Centre?
Voice	No. You've got the wrong number.
Anja	Oh, I'm sorry.
Voice	That's all right.
Anja	(dials the same number again)
Voice	Hello.
Anja	Oh! I'm so sorry, I've got the wrong number again.
Voice	Madam, what number are you dialling?
Anja	Two three three seven four six two zero.
Voice	That's the number all right, but there is no centre or anything of the kind here. This is my home number. Why don't you check the number before you dial? You just keep ringing up here again and again.

13.2   टेलीफ़ोन पर जानकारी हासिल करना

36

नृत्य महोत्सव के लिए टिकट

| आवाज़ | संगीत नाटक अकादमी के कथक केंद्र में आपका स्वागत है। आप क़तार |

में हैं। कृपया प्रतीक्षा कीजिए।

कार्यकर्ता	कथक केंद्र। नमस्ते।
आन्या	नमस्ते। मैं कथक महोत्सव के लिए टिकट ख़रीदना चाहती हूँ। आप मुझे बता सकते हैं कि आप के पास टिकट अभी मिल रहे हैं?
कार्यकर्ता	कृपया लाइन पर रहिए, मैं देखता हूँ। आप को कौन-से दिन का टिकट चाहिए?
आन्या	अगर हो सके तो तीनों दिन के दो-दो टिकट।
कार्यकर्ता	पहले और दूसरे दिन यानी तेरह फ़रवरी और चौदह फ़रवरी के टिकट अभी बाकी हैं, लेकिन आख़िरी दिन के जितने टिकट हमारे पास थे, वे सब बिक चुके हैं। हो सकता है कि हमारे किसी और टिकट बिक्री केंद्र में अभी हों।
आन्या	क्या कॉटेज इम्पोरियम में पंद्रह फ़रवरी के टिकट अभी होंगे?
कार्यकर्ता	यह तो आप को वहीं पूछना होगा।
आन्या	क्या मैं फ़ोन पर ही अपने नाम पर टिकट अलग रखवा सकती हूँ?
कार्यकर्ता	जी नहीं, यह सुविधा उपलब्ध नहीं है। टिकट हाथ के हाथ ही बिकते हैं।
आन्या	आप के यहाँ टिकट की बिक्री कब से कब तक होती है?
कार्यकर्ता	टिकट हमारे कार्यालय के काम के समय में मिलेंगे यानी सोमवार से शनिवार सुबह दस बजे से लेकर शाम पाँच बजे तक।
आन्या	माफ़ कीजिए, मैं समझ नहीं पाई। क्या आप समय फिर से बता सकते हैं?
कार्यकर्ता	हाँ, क्यों नहीं। हमारे कार्यालय के काम के समय है सोमवार से शनिवार सुबह दस बजे से लेकर शाम पाँच बजे तक।
आन्या	धन्यवाद।

13.2   Getting information on the phone

Tickets for a dance festival

Recording	Welcome to the Kathak Centre of the Music and Theatre Academy. You are currently in a queue. Please hold the line.
Clerk	Kathak Centre. Good morning.
Anja	Good morning. I would like to buy tickets for the Kathak festival. Could you tell me if they are still available with you?

Clerk	Please hold the line, I'll check. Which day do you want tickets for?
Anja	Two tickets each for all three days, if possible.
Clerk	We still have tickets left for the first and second day, that is, for the 3rd and 4th of February, but the tickets we had here for the last day are sold out. They might be available at another of our ticket sale outlets.
Anja	Would the Cottage Emporium still have tickets for 15th February?
Clerk	I'm afraid you'll have to ask there directly.
Anja	Can I reserve tickets in my name on the phone?
Clerk	I'm sorry but we don't offer this service. Tickets are sold only on-the-spot.
Anja	What are the opening hours of the ticket sales counter?
Clerk	Tickets can be bought during office hours, that is, Monday to Friday from 10 in the morning to 5 in the evening.
Anja	Pardon me, I didn't get that. Could you repeat the office hours, please?
Clerk	Certainly. Our office hours are Monday to Friday from 10 o'clock in the morning to 5 o'clock in the evening.
Anja	Thank you.

शब्दावली   Glossary

13.1 ग़लत नंबर मिलना: बदला हुआ टेलीफ़ोन नंबर
13.1 Dialling the wrong number: a changed telephone number

ग़लत wrong
आवाज़ f a voice
शिक्षण m teaching, instruction
नंबर m मिलाना to dial a telephone
                number

क्षमा कीजिए excuse/pardon me, sorry
बार-बार again and again, repeatedly
फ़ोन करना to ring up

13.2 टेलीफ़ोन पर जानकारी हासिल करना: नृत्य महोत्सव के लिए टिकट
13.2 Getting information on the phone: tickets for a dance festival

नाटक m a drama, a play
अकादमी f an academy
स्वागत m a welcome
क़तार f a line, a queue, a row
प्रतीक्षा f wait
  प्रतीक्षा करना to wait for
लाइन f telephone a line, a connection
बाक़ी होना to be left, to remain

आख़िरी last, final
बिक चुकना to be sold (out)
टिकट बिक्री केंद्र m a ticket sale centre/
                    a booth/an outlet
रखवाना to cause to be kept
सुविधा f a facility, a service,
         a convenience,
उपलब्ध available
हाथ के हाथ on-the-spot, directly
कार्यालय m an office

14
लड़ाई-झगड़ा, मुठभेड़
Fights and disputes

14.1 अपना पीछा छुड़ाना

चिपकू बेचनेवाले से अपना पिंड छुड़ाना

बेचनेवाला	मैडम, पश्मीना शॉल लेंगी?
पल्लवी	नहीं।
बेचनेवाला	हमारी दुकान उधर है। सब कश्मीर का माल है, बिलकुल ए-वन माल!
पल्लवी	होगा, मगर मुझे नहीं चाहिए।
बेचनेवाला	कश्मीरी गलीचे, दरियाँ?
पल्लवी	कहा न, नहीं चाहिए।
बेचनेवाला	टोकरियाँ, नक्काशी वाली पेटियाँ?
पल्लवी	नहीं! मुझे तंग मत करो।
बेचनेवाला	आ के देखिए तो, मैडम, देखना का कुछ नहीं लगता।
पल्लवी	देखो, मेरा सिर मत खाओ!

बेचनेवाला	एक बार दुकान में तो चलिए ...
पल्लवी	तुम तो बस हाथ धो के पीछे पड़ गए हो! बात समझ नहीं आती? अपना रास्ता नापो!
बेचनेवाला	आप के लिए अच्छा दाम लगाएँगे।
पल्लवी	मेरा पीछा छोड़ते हो या नहीं?
बेचनेवाला	मैडम, मैडम बात तो सुनो ...
पल्लवी	तुम्हारी यह मजाल! हाथ मत लगाओ मुझे! दफ़ा हो जाओ!

14.1   Getting rid of someone

Shaking off a pushy salesman

Vendor	Want a Pashmina shawl, Madam?
Pallavi	No.
Vendor	Our shop is over there. All our goods are from Kashmir, absolutely A-1 stuff!
Pallavi	It may be, but I don't want it.
Vendor	Carpets from Kashmir, rugs?
Pallavi	I just said, didn't I, I don't want anything.
Vendor	Baskets, carved boxes?
Pallavi	No! Don't pester me.
Vendor	Just come and take a look, Madam, looking is free of charge.
Pallavi	Look here, stop badgering me.
Vendor	Just come to the shop once…
Pallavi	You're getting on my nerves! Don't you understand? Go away!
Vendor	We'll give you a good price…
Pallavi	Will you stop hassling me!
Vendor	Madam, madam, just listen…
Pallavi	How dare you! Don't touch me! Get lost!

14.2   सड़क पर लड़ाई

ड्राइवर से कहा-सुनी

| पल्लवी | ऐ, क्या कर रहे हो? दिखता नहीं है? लड़ते-लड़ते बची है गाड़ी! |

ड्राइवर	ओ मैडम, बिना इंडिकेटर दिए गाड़ी घुमा दी। तेरे बाप की सड़क है क्या?
पल्लवी	ज़बान संभाल के बात करो! तमीज़ नहीं है क्या?
ड्राइवर	मुझे तमीज़ सिखाएगी? पहले खुद गाड़ी चलाना तो सीख ले!
पल्लवी	ग़लती तुम्हारी थी, तुम लाल बत्ती पर चल दिए। ऊपर से तू-तड़ाक कर रहे हो? अगर मेरी गाड़ी को खरोंच आती, तो फ़ौरन पुलिस बुलाकर तुम्हारी मरम्मत करवा देती।
ड्राइवर	ओय, क्या समझ रखा है अपने-आप को!
पल्लवी	बदतमीज़ कहीं के! चलो अब गाड़ी हटाओ — पीछे सारी ट्रैफ़िक रोक रखी है।
ड्राइवर	तू होती कौन है मुझे बताने वाली?
पल्लवी	देखिए भाईसाहब, आप अपने ड्राइवर को समझाइए। शरीफ़ लोगों के साथ गाली-गलौज करना ठीक नहीं है। और अपनी गाड़ी ज़रा हट-वाइए। शुक्रिया।

14.2   A confrontation on the road

An argument with a driver

Pallavi	Hey, what are you doing? Can't you see? Your car almost banged into mine!
Driver	Hey, lady, you turned without using the indicator. Think the road belongs to you?
Pallavi	Mind your language! Do you have no manners?
Driver	You'll teach me manners, will you? Better learn to drive first!
Pallavi	The fault was yours, you just jumped a red light. And on top of that you give me this backchat? If I'd got as much a scratch on my car, I'd have called the police and got them to knock some sense into you.
Driver	Hey, just who do think you are?
Pallavi	Ill-mannered lout! Come on now, get your car out of the way – you're holding up the entire traffic behind us.
Driver	Who the hell are you to tell me what to do?
Pallavi	Excuse me, sir, please give your driver a talking-to. It isn't right to use offensive language with respectable people. And please have your car moved out of the way. Thank you.

शब्दावली   Glossary

14.1 अपना पीछा छुड़ाना: चिपकू बेचनेवाले से अपना पिंड छुड़ाना
14.1 Getting rid of someone: Shaking off a pushy salesman

पिंड/पीछा छुड़ाना to get rid of
पश्मीना *m* pashmina, fine cashmere
शॉल *m* a shawl
कश्मीर *m* Kashmir (a federal state in
          North India)
माल *m* wares, goods
गलीचा *m* a carpet
दरी *f* a cotton rug, a carpet
टोकरी *f* a basket
नक्काशी *f* carving
पेटी *f* a box, a case
तंग करना to pester, to badger

सिर खाना to get on someone's nerves
हाथ धो के पीछे पड़ना to pursue someone
          relentlessly/to hound
समझना to understand
नापना to measure
 अपना रास्ता नापो Go away! Make
          yourself scarce!
पीछा छोड़ना to leave alone
मजाल *f* nerve, courage
 तुम्हारी यह मजाल! How dare you!
हाथ लगाना to touch
दफ़ा हो जाओ! Get lost! Beat it!

14.2 सड़क पर लड़ाइ: ड्राइवर से कहा-सुनी
14.2 A confrontation on the road: an argument with a driver

लड़ाई *f* an altercation, a fight, a quarrel
कहा-सुनी *f* a dispute, a wrangle,
          an argument
लड़ना 1. to collide 2. to fight, quarrel
बचना to be saved, to escape
इंडिकेटर *m* an indicator
घुमाना to turn something
तेरे बाप का *impolite* your personal
          property
ज़बान *f* 1. the tongue 2. a language
 ज़बान संभाल कर बात करो! mind/watch
          your language!
तमीज़ *f* courtesy, manners
सिखाना teach
ग़लती *f* a mistake

तू-तड़ाक *f* rudeness
खरोंच *f* a scratch, a graze
फ़ौरन immediately
मरम्मत *f* repair
मरम्मत करना *figurative* to give a good
          beating
समझना to consider, to perceive
बदतमीज़ rude, ill-mannered
कहीं का of unknown origin, strange
हटाना remove
पीछे behind
रोकना 1. to stop, halt 2. to obstruct
समझाना 1. to explain 2. to admonish
शरीफ़ noble, wellborn, refined
गाली-गलौज *f* abuse

15
लेखा-जोखा
A summing up

15.1   समय

वक़्त की पाबंदी

अजय   आन्या, तुम किस काम में जुटी हुई हो? हम लोग ठीक समय पर तो पहुँच
         जाएँगे?

आन्या   हाँ, हाँ, फ़िक्र मत करो, मैं दो मिनट में तैयार होती हूँ। कितने बजे हैं अभी?

अजय   सवा बारह ... नहीं, बारह बीस हो रहे हैं।

आन्या   ओहो, अभी तो बहुत वक़्त है। कार्यक्रम तो ढाई बजे शुरू होने वाला है न?

अजय   हाँ, लेकिन वहाँ पहुँचने में हमें आधा-पौना घंटा लग जाएगा। और ज़रा भी
         देर नहीं होनी चाहिए, नहीं तो मुझे बहुत शर्मिंदा होना पड़ेगा।

आन्या	कोई देर-वेर नहीं होगी, हम लोग ठीक उद्घाटन के समय पर पहुँच जाएँगे। तुम्हें तो पता ही है कि जर्मन लोगों की समय की पाबंदी दुनिया भर में मशहूर है!
अजय	देवी जी, उस से भी ज़्यादा मशहूर यह है कि औरतें सजने में घंटों लगा देती हैं।
आन्या	तुम नाहक़ घबरा रहे हो। हम लोग पौने दो बजे घर से निकलें?
अजय	मेरे ख़्याल से हमें डेढ़ बजे निकल जाना चाहिए। दस-पाँच मिनट जल्दी पहुँचने में कोई हर्ज नहीं है।
आन्या	अच्छा, तो मैं सवा बजे तक तैयार हो जाती हूँ।
अजय	हाँ, ठीक है। निकलते-निकलते फिर डेढ़ बज ही जाएँगे।
आन्या	कार्यक्रम चलेगा कब तक, कुछ मालूम है?
अजय	पहला हिस्सा अंदाज़न ढाई घंटे में ख़तम हो जाना चाहिए। फिर हम लोग चल सकते हैं क्योंकि दूसरे भाग से हमारा कोई मतलब नहीं है।
आन्या	अढ़ाई घंटे ... इस का मतलब कि हम लोग साढ़े छह-सात तक लौट आएँगे? मेरा अभी काफ़ी काम बाकी है।
अजय	सात बजे तक तो हर हालत में घर आ जाएँगे।

15.1   Time

Punctuality

Ajay	What work are you so engrossed in, Anja? We'll get there on time, won't we?
Anja	Yes, yes, don't worry, I'll be ready in a minute. What time is it now?
Ajay	A quarter past ... no, it's getting on for twenty past twelve.
Anja	Well then, there's plenty of time left. The programme begins at 2:30, doesn't it?
Ajay	Yes, but we'll need half or three quarters of an hour to get there. And we shouldn't be even a bit late, or it'll be most embarrassing for me.
Anja	We'll be nothing of the sort, we'll get there on the dot for the inauguration. You know very well that German punctuality is famous all over the world!
Ajay	Dear lady, even more famous is the fact that women take hours to get dressed.

Anja	You're getting worked up for nothing. Should we leave at a quarter to two?
Ajay	I think we should get out at half past one. There's no harm in getting there a few minutes early.
Anja	Fine, then I'll be ready by a quarter past one.
Ajay	Good. By the time we actually leave the house, it will be half past one anyway.
Anja	How long will the programme go on? Any idea?
Ajay	The first part should be over in about two and a half hours. Then we can leave, since the second part doesn't concern us.
Anja	Two and a half hours … that means we'll be back by six thirty, seven? I have quite a lot of work left.
Ajay	We'll be back home by seven at any rate.

15.2   अंकों का खेल

मुहावरे और लोकोक्तियाँ

आन्या	मुझे आप लोगों की मदद की ज़रूरत है। मैं एक लेख के लिए हिन्दी के कुछ मुहावरे इकट्ठा कर रही हूँ। आप मुझे कुछ-एक ऐसी कहावतें बता सकते हैं जो अंकों से संबंधित हों ?
राजन	शौक़ से। बस ज़रा सोचना पड़ेगा …। लोकोक्ति भी हो सकती है?
आन्या	जी हाँ, बिलकुल।
अजय	एक कहावत है: एक चुप हज़ार सुख।
आन्या	अच्छी है। यह तो आसानी से समझ में आ गया।
राजन	एक और एक ग्यारह होते हैं।
आन्या	मतलब?
राजन	मतलब मिल कर काम करने से शक्ति बढ़ती है।
अलका	दो कौड़ी का होना। यानी तुच्छ या नीच होना।
आन्या	इस के साथ कोई वाक्य?
अलका	उस दो कौड़ी के आदमी से मैं बात भी नहीं करती।
अजय	अब तीन से … तीन पाँच करना।
आन्या	तीन-पाँच? इस के क्या माने हैं?
अलका	तीन-पाँच करना माने बात बनाना या घुमा-फिरा कर बात करना।

अजय	हाँ, लेकिन इस का एक और मतलब भी है। वह है हुज्जत करना।
राजन	सात-पाँच करने के भी वही माने होते हैं।
आन्या	बहुत बढ़िया। जितनी जल्दी आप लोग बोल रहे है, उतनी जल्दी तो मैं लिख ही नहीं पा रही!
अलका	एक, दो, तीन हो गए, अब आई चार की बारी। चार सौ बीस। जो आदमी चार सौ बीस होता है वह चार सौ बीसी करता है।
आन्या	अरे हाँ, यह मुझे भी मालूम था, उस राज कपूर की फ़िल्म की वजह से।
अजय	अब आए पाँच पर। तो यह लो: पाँचों उँगलियाँ घी में होना।
आन्या	घी में ... क्या इस के माने हैं बहुत अच्छी स्थिति में होना?
राजन	बिलकुल ठीक अंदाज़ा लगाया आपने!
आन्या	जर्मन में भी इस से मिलता-जुलता एक मुहावरा है। बस हम लोग घी के बजाय मक्खन का उपयोग करते है।
राजन	अब छह पर पहुँचे। तो लेते हैं: छक्के छूटना। यानी हिम्मत हारना।
अलका	एक और मतलब भी है न? शेर को देख कर मेरे छक्के छूट गए, यानी मेरी बुद्धी चकरा गई।
आन्या	यह मैं न सोच पाती। सात हो चुका है, आठ से भी कोई मुहावरा है?
अजय	हाँ, कई हैं। जैसे कि — आठ-आठ आँसू रोना।
अलका	यह कहावत तो मैं भी पहली बार सुन रही हूँ। आठ आँसू ज़्यादा होते हैं कि कम? ज़्यादा होंगे।
अजय	बिलकुल ठीक, आपने परीक्षा पास कर ली।
आन्या	तो आठ-आठ आँसू रोना का मतलब है बहुत ज़्यादा रोना?
राजन	जी। नौ से मुझे एक बहुत आम इस्तेमाल की कहावत याद आ रही है। नौ दो ग्यारह होना।
आन्या	नौ दो ग्यारह? मैंने अभी तक नहीं सुना है।
राजन	शायद इस वाक्य से इस का अर्थ स्पष्ट हो जाएगा: पुलिस को देखते ही चोर नौ दो ग्यारह हो गए।
आन्या	भाग गए? ग़ायब हो गए?
अलका	एकदम सही। आप की हिन्दी तो दिन दूनी रात चौगुनी तरक़्क़ी कर रही है!
आन्या	बहुत बहुत शुक्रिया। आप लोगों की सहायता से तो मेरे लेख में चार चाँद लग जाएँगे!

15.2   A game of numbers

Idioms and proverbs

Anja	I wonder if you could all help me. I'm collecting some Hindi idioms for an article. Could you give me some expressions connected with numbers?
Rajan	With pleasure. Need to think a bit... Can it be a proverb, too?
Anja	By all means.
Ajay	There's an idiom that goes: one silence, a thousand joys.
Anja	That's nice. That was easy to understand.
Rajan	One and one makes eleven.
Anja	What does it mean?
Rajan	It means unity is strength.
Alka	Be twopenny worth. It means: to be worthless or contemptible.
Anja	Could I have a sentence with this phrase?
Alka	I don't even talk to that worthless man.
Ajay	And now with three... to make three and five.
Anja	Three and five? What does that mean?
Alka	Making three and five means telling tall tales or prevaricating.
Ajay	That's right, but it also has another meaning. That is arguing or wrangling.
Ajay	Making sevens and fives also has the same meaning.
Anja	Great! You are all going so fast that I can barely manage to jot down everything!
Alka	We've done one, two and three, now it's four's turn. Four hundred twenty. A person who is a 420 swindles and cheats.
Anja	Oh, yes, I knew that because of that Raj Kapoor film.
Ajay	Now we come to five. Here you go: to have all five fingers in ghee.
Anja	In ghee ... does that mean, to be in a very comfortable situation?
Rajan	You guessed absolutely right!
Anja	There's a similar saying in German, only we say 'butter' instead of ghee.
Rajan	Now we've got to six. Let's take: to miss the sixes. Which means, to lose heart.
Alka	There's another meaning, too, isn't there? I missed my sixes on seeing the lion, which means I was dazed.
Anja	I'd never have guessed that. Seven is done, is there an idiom with eight as well?

Ajay	Yes, several. For instance – to weep eight tears.
Alka	This is an expression that even I am hearing for the first time. Are eight tears only a few or many? Many, probably.
Ajay	Exactly! You've passed the test.
Anja	So to weep eight tears means to weep copiously?
Rajan	Yes. With nine, there is a very common expression that comes to mind. To be nine-two-eleven.
Anja	Nine-two-eleven? Never heard that one before.
Rajan	Perhaps this sentence will make the meaning clear: as soon as they saw the police, the thieves did a nine-two-eleven.
Anja	Ran away? Vanished without a trace?
Alka	Precisely. Your Hindi is progessing by leaps and bounds!
Anja	Many, many thanks. Your help will improve my article four-fold!

शब्दावली Glossary

15.1 समय: वक़्त की पाबंदी
15.1 Time: punctuality

लेख़ा-जेख़ा *m* an account, a reckoning, assessment
   लेख़ा-जेख़ा करना to reassess, to take stock
जुटना to be involved/absorbed
समय *m* time
फ़िक्र/फ़िकर *f* concern, anxiety
कितने बजे हैं? what time is it?
सवा बारह a quarter past twelve
बारह बीस twenty minutes past twelve
कार्यक्रम *m* a programme
ढाई/अढ़ाई two and a half
ढाई बजे half past two; two-thirty
आधा घंटा half an hour
पौना less by a quarter
पौना घंटा three quarters of an hour
शर्मिंदा/ शरमिंदा होना embarrassed; ashamed

उद्घाटन *m* inauguration, opening
सजना to dress up, to be adorned
नाहक़ needlessly, without good cause
घबराना...to be perturbed/agitated
ख़याल *m* an opinion; a thought
  मेरे ख़याल से in my opinion
डेढ़ one and a half
डेढ़ बजे half past one, one thirty
हर्ज *m* harm, loss, damage
हिस्सा *m* part
अंदाज़न approximately
ख़तम/ख़त्म होना to finish
भाग *m* part
मतलब *m* purpose/meaning, sense
अढ़ाई/ढाइ two and a half
साढ़े छह six and a half
साढ़े छह बजे six thirty
हर हालत में in any case, at any rate

15.2 अंकों का खेल: मुहावरे और लोकोक्तियाँ
15.2 A game of numbers: idioms and proverbs

अंक *m* a number, a figure
मुहावरा *m* an idiom, a current expression
लोकोक्ति *f* a proverb
इकट्ठा करना to collect
कहावत *f* a proverb, a saying
शौक़ से gladly, with pleasure
चुप *f* silence, quiet
हज़ार *m* a thousand

आसानी *f* ease
शक्ति *f* power, strength
कौड़ी *f* a small shell, a cowrie
तुच्छ worthless, contemptible
नीच base, mean
वाक्य *m* a sentence
बात बनाना to invent a story
हुज्जत *f* an argument, an objection (esp. frivolous)

बारी *f* a time, a turn
उँगली / अँगुली *f* a finger
घी *m* clarified butter
अंदाज़ा *m* a rough estimate, a guess
स्पष्ट clear
मिलता-जुलता similar
मक्ख़न *m* butter
उपयोग *m* use
छक्का *m* a six (in cards, dice, cricket)
हिम्मत *f* spirit, courage
   हिम्मत *f* हारना to become dispirited,
            to lose heart

बुद्धी *f* intelligence, mind
चकराना to spin, to whirl; to be
            perplexed/confused
आँसू *m* a tear
रोना to cry, to weep
अर्थ *m* a meaning
ग़ायब disappeared, vanished
दूना twice as much
चौगुना fourfold

मुहावरे और लोकोक्तियाँ
Idioms and proverbs

एक चुप हज़ार सुख	Silence is golden
एक और एक ग्यारह होते हैं	There is strength in unity; united we stand, divided we fall
दो कौड़ी का होना	to be a worthless/contemptible person
तीन पाँच करना	1. to dispute or to quarrel 2. to practise trickery
चार सौ बीस	a fraudster/a swindler
चार सौ बीसी करना	to cheat, swindle, defraud
पाँचों उँगलियाँ घी में होना	to live in the lap of luxury; to revel in wealth, or in material comforts
छक्के छूटना	1. to lose heart 2. to be disconcerted, bewildered
आठ-आठ आँसू रोना	to be in floods of tears
नौ-दो-ग्यारह होना	to vanish, disappear; to make oneself scarce
दिन दूना रात चौगुना करना	to develop or progress at accelerating speed, by leaps and bounds
चार चाँद लगना	to be enhanced /improved in attractiveness, quality, value, etc.

Hindi–English glossary

अ

अंक *m* a number, a figure

अंगूर *m* a grape

अंजीर *f* a fig

अंत *m* the end

अंतर *m* difference

अंदर within, inside

अंदाज़ा *m* a rough estimate, a guess

अंदाज़न approximately

अंधा-धुंध thoughtless, headlong

अंधेरी dark

अकादमी *f* an academy

अकेले alone, on one's own

अकेले पड़ना to grow lonely

अक़्लमंद intelligent

अक्सर often

अख़बार *m* a newspaper

अख़बारवाला *m* a paperboy

अगर if

अगला next, following

अचानक suddenly, by chance

अच्छा 1. good, pleasant, fine
2. *interjection* Good! Well!

अच्छा लगना to please

अच्छे से अच्छा the very best

अटूट unfailing, inexhaustible

अटैची *f* a suitcase, an attaché case

अढ़ाई / ढाइ two and a half

अतिरिक्त extra, additionally

के अतिरिक्त apart from,
in addition to

अत्यंत extremely

अदरक *m* ginger

अद्भुत astonishing, remarkable

अधिक more

अधिकांश *m, adj, adv.* a majority, the
majority of, on the whole

अध्ययन *m* study, research

अध्यापन *m* teaching

अनगिनत innumerable, countless

अनजान unknown

अनार *m* Bengal light: a firework

अनुकृति *f* a replica

अनुमान *m* a guess, an estimate

अनुमान लगाना to suppose, to estimate

अनुवाद *m* a translation

अनुसंधान *m* research

(के) अनुसार according (to), following

अनेक several

अनोखा uncommon, unusual

अन्य other, different

अप्रसन्न displeased

अफ़सोस *m* sorrow, regret

अफ़सोस की बात है (it is) a pity

अब now, just now, nowadays

अभिनंदन *m* करना to greet

अभिभाषण *m* a formal address

अभियान *m* a campaign

अभियुक्त *m* a culprit, the accused

अभी just now, immediately, yet, still

अमचूर *m* dried mango powder

अमरीका *m* America

अमावस्या *f* the night of the new moon

अयोग्य incapable, incompetent

अयोध्या *f* a North Indian town, in the
epic poem *Ramayana* the
birthplace of the god Rama

अरसा / अर्सा *m* a space of time

अरसे से / अर्से से for a long (past) time

अरे *interjection* Hey! Oh!

अरे वाह! Bravo! Wow! Splendid!

अर्थ *m* a meaning
अर्थ-शास्त्र *m* economics
अलग 1. apart, separately 2. different
  अलग–अलग different, a variety of
(के) अलावा in addition to, apart from
अवकाश *m*/फुरसत *m* leisure
अवधि *f* a set time, a period
अवश्य certainly, of course
अवसर *m* an occasion, an opportunity
अवसर/मौक़ा हाथ से जाने न देना to not
                 miss an opportunity/
                 a chance
अश्रांत tireless
असंतुष्ट dissatisfied, displeased
असंतुष्टि *f* dissatisfaction
असंभव impossible
असरदार effective
असल में in fact
  असलियत *f* truth, fact, reality
अस्पताल *m* a hospital

आ

आँकड़ा *m* an estimate, a figure,
              statistics
आँच *f* a flame, heat
आंटी *f* aunty; form of address used by
      children to show respect
आँसू *m* a tear
आइस-क्रीम *f* ice cream
आख़िर in the end, after all
आख़िरी last, final
आगे in front, ahead
आगे–पीछे front and back, around
आज today
आजकल nowadays, recently
ऑटो *m* an autorickshaw
आठ eight
आतंकवाद *m* terrorism
आतंकवादी *m* a terrorist
आतिशबाज़ी *f* fireworks

आतुर impatient
आत्मघात *m* a suicide
आदमी *m* a man, a person
आदर्शवादी idealistic
आदेश *m* an order, a directive
आधा घंटा *m* half an hour
आनंद *m* enjoyment, delight
  आनंद लेना to enjoy to the full
आना to come
आप *honorific* 1. you 2. he/she
आप से आप of its own accord
आपस में among themselves, mutually
  आपस में बनना to get on with someone
आभारी grateful, obliged
आम *m* a mango
आम common, general
  आम आदमी *m* the common man
  आम जनता *f* the common people
  आम तौर पर/से usually, in general
आमदनी *f* an income
आयोजन *m* organisation, arrangement
  आयोजित करना to organise
आरक्षण *m* reservation (of a seat)
  आरक्षण-सूची *f* a (train) reservation list
आरती *f* a Hindu ceremony performed
         by moving a plate holding a
         lamp, incense, etc. in circles
         in front of a deity or person
आराम *m* rest, ease, comfort
  आराम *m* करना to rest, to relax
  आराम से 1. at/with ease
             2. unhurriedly, gently
आरामदेह comfortable
आर्डर *m* an order (for food or drink)
आर्थिक financial, economic, monetary
आलीशान magnificent
आलू *m* a potato
आवाज़ *f* 1. a voice 2. a noise 3. a sound
आवेदन-पत्र *m* an application
आशीर्वाद *m* a blessing

आस–पास in the vicinity, round about
आसान easy, simple
आसानी *f* ease
आहार *m* food
  आहार विषाक्तन *m* food poisoning

इ

इंडिकेटर *m* an indicator (on a vehicle)
इंगलैंड *m* England
इंतज़ार *m*/इंतज़ारी *f* wait, expectation
इकट्ठा (gathered/taken) together
इकट्ठा करना to collect
इकलौती बेटी *f* an only daughter
इच्छा *f* a wish
  इच्छा पूरी करना to fulfil a wish
इतना as much/many as this
इतवार *m* Sunday
इतिहास *m* history
इधर here, over here
इम्तहान *m* an examination, a test
इरादा *m* an intention, a desire
इर्द–गिर्द all around
इलाज *m* 1. a remedy, cure 2. treatment
इलायची *f* a cardamom
इलेक्ट्रोलाइट *m* oral rehydration salts
इसलिए for this reason, therefore
इस्तीफ़ा *m* a resignation
  इस्तीफ़ा देना to resign
इस्तेमाल *m* a use, exercise
  इस्तेमाल करना to use

ई

ईद *f* Id/Eid, a Muslim holiday
  ईद का चाँद something rarely seen

उ

उँगली /अँगुली *f* a finger
उचित appropriate, fitting
उच्च शिक्षा *f* higher education

उज्जवलित lit up, aglow, ablaze
उठना to get up, to stand up
उड़ीसा *m* Orissa, a state in East India
उतरना to come down, to sink/subside
उतारना 1. to let down/drop off
          2. to take off (clothes/shoes)
उत्तर प्रदेश/यूपी/उ.प्र. *m* Uttar Pradesh,
                       a state in North India
उत्सव *m* a festival
उत्सुक eager, keen
  उत्सुकता *f* eagerness, keenness
उद्देश्य *m* an intention, a purpose
उद्घाटन *m* an inauguration, an opening
उन्नति *f* improvement, progress
  उन्नति होना to prosper, to progress
उन्माद *m* madness, a frenzy, passion
उपन्यास *m* a novel
उपयोग *m* use
उपलक्ष्य *m* an occasion
उपलब्ध available
उपलब्धि *f* an achievement
उपहार *m* a gift
उपाधि *f* a title, a degree
उपाय *m* a means, a measure, recourse
उबला हुआ boiled
उबालना to boil
उमंग *f* rapture, rejoicing, elation
उम्दा excellent
उम्मीद *f* hope, expectation
उम्मीदवार *m* a candidate, an applicant
उम्र *f* age
उलटी *f* vomiting, nausea

ऊ

ऊट-पटाँग nonsensical, absurd
ऊपर 1. on top 2. over, overhead
  ऊपर वाला *m* situated or dwelling
                  above, *also* God
  के ऊपर 1. over, above 2. on top of

ऊबना to be dispirited, to be bored
ऊल-जलूल silly, stupid, pointless

ए

एक-आध one or two, a few
एकदम completely
एकाएक suddenly, unexpectedly
एक्स्प्रेस *f* an express train
एतराज़ *m* an objection
एम.ए. *m* an MA, a master's degree
एम.टेक. *m* a master's degree in
technology
एम.बी.ए. *m* an MBA

ऐ

ऐंटीबायोटिक *m* an antibiotic
ऐंठन *f* cramps, colic, a griping pain
ऐतिहासिक historic
ऐसा of this sort, like this
ऐसा-वैसा nondescript, commonplace

ओ

ओर *f* a side, a direction
ओवरटाइम *m* overtime
ओहो *interjection* oh!

औ

औरत *f* a woman
औषधालय / दवा-ख़ाना *m* a chemist
औषधि / दवा *f* a medicine

क

कंपार्टमेंट *m* a compartment in a train
कई several, a few
कई दिनों से a few/several days since
कटवाना to cause to be cut
कट्टर fanatical, unyielding, strict
कट्टरपंथी *m* a fanatic

कठिनाई *f* a difficulty
कड़ा 1. harsh, severe, 2. tough, strong
कढ़ाई *f* embroidery
कतली *f* a type of sweet in thin slices
कतार *f* a line, a queue, a row
कथक / कत्थक *m* a form of Indian
classical dance
कदम *m* a step, a pace
दो / चार कदम पर a stone's throw
from
कपड़ा *m* 1. clothes, a garment 2. cloth
कभी sometime
कभी कभी sometimes
कभी नहीं never
कम 1. little, few 2. less
कम करना to reduce, decrease
कम से कम at least
कमबख़्त wretched
कमरा *m* a room
कमाई *f* earnings
कमाना to earn
कमाल *m* a miracle, a wonderful thing
कमाल का wonderful
कमी *f* a deficit, a shortage
कमीज़ *f* a shirt/a tunic
कम्प्यूटर विज्ञान *m* computer science
कर पाना to manage to do
करवाना to have or to get done
क़रीब-क़रीब almost
कर्मचारी *m* an employee, a worker
कल 1. tomorrow 2. yesterday
कल मिलेंगे see you tomorrow
कला *f* art
कलाई *f* the wrist
कलाकंद *m* a sweet made of cream
cheese and sugar
कलाकार *m* an artist, a performer
कलाकृति *f* a work of art
कल्याण-संस्था *f* a welfare organisation

कविता *f*   a poem, poetry

कश्मीर *m*   Kashmir (a federal state in North India)

कष्ट *m*   inconvenience, trouble

कसर *f* नहीं रखना   leave nothing wanting

कहना *m*   advice

कहना   to say, to speak, to tell

कहानी *f*   a story

कहा-सुनी *f*   a dispute, awrangle

कहावत *f*   a proverb, a saying

कहीं   somewhere, anywhere

   कहीं का   of unknown origin, strange

काउंटर *m*   a counter (sales/cash, etc.)

काजू *m*   a cashew nut

काटना   to cut

काफ़ी   1. enough 2. quite, fairly

काबुली चना *m*   a chickpea

काबू *m*   control

काम *m*   work, occupation, activity

   काम छोड़ना   to resign a post

   काम पर जाना   to go to work

कामचोर *m, adj.*   idle, an idler, a shirker

कामना *f*   a wish, a desire

कामयाब   successful

कारण *m*   a cause, a reason

कार्तिक / कार्त्तिक *m*   the 8th month of the Hindu lunar year (October-November)

कार्यकर्ता *m*   a worker, an official

कार्यक्रम *m*   a programme, a timetable

कार्यभार *m*   workload

कार्यशाला *f*   a workshop

कार्यालय *m*   an office

कॉलेज *m*   a college

काली मिर्च *f*   black pepper

किच-किच *f*   wrangling

कितना   1. how much/many 2. how..!

   कितने बजे   at what time

किताब *f*   a book

किताब-घर *m*   a bookshop

किराया *m*   charge for rent, hire or lease

   किराए पर लेना   to take on rent/hire

किला *m*   a fort, a castle

किलो *m*   a kilogramme

किलोमीटर   a kilometre

किसी भी तरह का/की   any kind of

की ओर से   on behalf of

कीर्तन *m*   a hymn

कुँवारी /कुँआरी *f*   an unmarried woman

कुछ   something, some, a little

   कुछ नहीं   nothing

कुटिया *f*   a hut

कुटीर उद्योग *m*   a cottage industry

कुरता/कुर्ता *m*   a loose, collarless shirt

कुरती *f*   a blouse, a short tunic

कुर्सी /कुरसी   a chair, a seat

कुल   entire, the whole, total

   कुल मिलाकर   altogether

कुलफ़ी *f*   Indian ice cream

कुली *m*   a porter

कुल्हड़ *m*   an earthenware cup

कुहनी *f*   the elbow

कृपया / कृपा *f* करके   kindly, please

केंद्र *m*   a centre

केंद्रीय   central

केला *m*   a banana

केवल   only

केसर *m*   saffron

कैमरा *m*   a camera

कोई बात नहीं   no matter; that's all right

कोना *m*   a corner

कोशिश *f*   an effort, an attempt

कौड़ी *f*   a small shell, a cowrie

कौन   who?

   कौन-सा   which?

क्या कहना!   *interjection* an expression of great admiration

क्यों   why

क्रिकेट प्रेमी *m* a cricket fan

क्रीम *f* a cream, an ointment

क्रेडिट-कार्ड *m* a credit card

क्लिनिक *f* a clinic

क्षमा *f* forgiveness, pardon

   क्षमा कीजिए excuse/pardon me, sorry

क्षेत्र *m* an area, a sphere of action

ख

ख़चाख़च crowded, packed tightly

ख़तम/ख़त्म होना to finish

ख़तरा *m* danger

ख़दबद करना to boil, to simmer

ख़बर *f* news, information

ख़याल *m* 1. an opinion 2. a thought

   मेरे ख़याल से I think, in my opinion

   ख़याली पुलाव पकाना to build castles in

                  the air

ख़राब 1. bad 2. defective, damaged

ख़रीदना to buy

ख़रोंच *f* a scratch, a graze

ख़र्च करना to spend

ख़ाँसना to cough

ख़ाँसी *f* a cough

ख़ाना *m* 1. food 2. to eat*(verb)*

ख़ाली 1. empty, free 2. only, merely

ख़ास 1. special, particular 2.choice

   ख़ासकर in particular, especially

   ख़ास तौर से *m* in particular, especially

   ख़ासियत *f* speciality, special quality

खिड़की *f* a window

खिलाड़ी *m* a player

खिलाना to cause/invite to eat, to feed

(के) ख़िलाफ़ against

ख़ीर *f* a rice pudding

ख़ीरा *m* a cucumber

ख़ुद self (myself, himself, itself, etc.)

खुलना to be open(ed), to come loose

ख़ुश रहो may you always be happy!

ख़ुशख़बरी *f* good news

ख़ुशी *f* happiness, pleasure

ख़ून *m* blood

ख़ूब 1. fine, splendid 2. very much,

          lots (of)

ख़ूबसूरत beautiful

खेल *m* a game

   खेल-कूद *m* sport, games

ख़ैरियत *f* 1. well-being 2. good fortune

ख़ोया/ख़ोआ *m* thickened milk

ख़ोज *f* 1. search 2. enquiry

ख़ोलना to open

ख़ौफ़नाक fearsome, terrifying

ग

गंदा dirty, filthy

गंभीर serious, thoughtful

गठजोड़/गँठजोड़ *m* an alliance

गड़बड़ *m, f*/गड़बड़ी *f* disorder, confusion

गड्डी *f* a heap, a pile

गढ़वाल *m* Garhwal, a mountainous

          region in North India

गणेश *m* Ganesh(a), the elephant-

          headed Hindu god of wisdom

गतिविधि *f* an activity

गरम hot, warm

गरम मसाला *m* an aromatic mixture of

          ground spices

गरमी/गर्मी *f* 1. heat 2. summer

गर्भ-गृह *m* the inner sanctum of a

          temple

गर्व *m* pride

ग़लत wrong

ग़लती *f* a mistake

गला *m* 1. the throat 2. the neck

   गला ख़राब होना to have a sore throat

गलीचा/ग़ालीचा *m* a small carpet

गाज *m* a thunderbolt, lightning

गाड़ी *f* 1. a train 2. any vehicle: car, etc.

   गाड़ी चलाना to drive

   (गाड़ी) खड़ी करना to park

गाना *m* 1. a song, singing
2. *(verb)* to sing
गायक *m* a singer
गाली-गलौज *f* abuse
गिनती *f* counting
गिने-चुने selected
गिरजाघर/गिरजा *m* a church
गुट *m* a group, a faction
गुणी talented, excellent, worthy
गुनगुना lukewarm, tepid
गुरु *m* a teacher
गुलाबी pink
गुस्ल-ख़ाना *m* a bathroom
गूंज *f* reverberation, resonance
गृहप्रवेश *m* a house-warming ceremony
गृहमंत्री *m* the home minister
ग़ैर- un-, non-, other
 ग़ैर-सरकारी non-governmental
 ग़ैर-सरकारी संगठन *m* an NGO
 ग़ैर-हिन्दु *m* a non-Hindu
गैस *f* gas
गोभी *f* a cauliflower
गोल चक्कर *m* a roundabout,
 a traffic circle
गोली *f* a tablet, a pill
गोश्त *m* meat, *also* mutton
ग्यारह eleven
ग्रहण *m* acquisition, acceptance
 ग्रहण करना to accept, to obtain
ग्राम *m* a gramme
ग्रामीण rural

घ

घंटा *m* an hour
घंटी *f* a bell
घटना *f* a happening, an incident
घबराना/घबड़ाना to be perturbed
घरवाले *pl* a family, family members
घायल wounded, injured

घिरना to be surrounded
घी *m* clarified butter
घुमाना 1. to turn (something) 2. to take
 someone out/round
घूमना-फिरना to roam, to tour
घोलना to dissolve
घोषणा *f* an announcement

च

चकराना to spin; to be perplexed
चक्कर आना to grow dizzy
चखना to taste
चचेरा भाई *m* a cousin (father's
 brother's son)
चढ़ाना to offer to a deity
चप्पल *f* an open shoe, a sandal
चमचागिरी *f* flattery
चमत्कारी astonishing, wonderful
चम्मच *m* a spoon
चरमपंथी *m* an extremist
चर्चा *f* a discussion, a talk
चलना 1. to go, to move 2. to start, to
 depart, to set out 3. to endure
चलाना 1. to stir 2. to drive, to cause to
 move or go
चहेता *m* a darling, a favourite
चाँद *m* the moon
चाचा *m* an uncle (father's younger
 brother)
चाची *f* an aunt (father's younger
 brother's wife)
चादर *f* a sheet
चापलूसी *f* flattery, sycophancy
चाबी *f* a key
चाय *f* tea
चार four
 चारों ओर all around, everywhere
चालक *m* a driver
चावल *m* rice
चाहना to wish, to ask for, to choose

चाहिये   should, is wanted/needful

चाहे... चाहे   whether ... or

चिंता *f*   concern, anxiety, worry

चिट्ठी *f*   a letter

चित्र-कला *f*   painting

चिपचिपा   sticky, clinging

चिप्पी *f*   a sticker

चीज़ *f*   a thing

चुकना   to be finished, completed

चुकाना   to settle, to pay

चुनना   to choose, to select

चुनाव *m*   an election

   चुनावी नतीजा *m*   election result

चुप   a silence, quiet

चूना   to drip, to leak

चेहरा *m*   a face, features

चैन *m*   ease of mind, peace, repose

चोट *f*   a wound, an injury, a bruise

चौकसी *f* बरतना   to be alert/vigilant

चौगुना   fourfold

चौपट करना   to ruin, to corrupt

छ

छपना   1. to be printed (cloth)
       2. to be printed/published

छाँह *f*   shade

छाती *f*   the chest

छात्रवृति *f*   a scholarship

छाना   to be spread

छिलना   to be scraped or grazed

छींटा *m*   a drop

   छींटा डालना   to sprinkle

छीलना   to skin, to peel, to pare

छुटकारा *m*   a relief, a release

   छुटकारा मिलना   to be freed, to get rid of

छुट्टी *f*   a holiday, a vacation, leave

   छुट्टी लेना   to take leave/a holiday

छुट्टे (पैसे)   small change

छूटना   to leave, to depart

छोटी-सी   small, little

छोड़ना   1. to give up, to resign
        2. to leave

छोले *pl*   chickpeas

ज

जँचना   to seem good, to suit

जगत् *m*   the world

जगमगाना   to glitter, to sparkle

जगह *f*   a place

जनता *f*   people, populace

जनवरी *f*   January

जनसत्ता *f*   the people's mandate: name
              of a Hindi daily newspaper

जन्माष्टमी *f*   a festival to celebrate the
                birth of the god Krishna

ज़बान *f*   1. the tongue 2. a language

   ज़बान संभाल कर बात करो!   mind your
                            language!

ज़माना *m*   a time, a period, the times

जयपुर   Jaipur (capital of the North
          Indian state of Rajasthan)

ज़रा   1. a little
       2. just: would you mind, please

ज़रूर   certainly, of course

   ज़रूरत *f*   a need, a necessity

   ज़रूरत होना   to be needed

जर्मन *m/f/adj.*   German

जर्मनी *m*   Germany

जलाना   to light

जल्दबाज़ी *f*   haste, hurry, impetuosity

जल्दी *f*   1. speed 2. haste, impetuosity

   जल्दी पड़ी होना   to be in a hurry

   जल्दी में होना   to be in a hurry

जाँच *f*   an investigation, an enquiry,
            an examination

जाति *f*   a caste

जान *f*   a life

   जान देना   to dote (on/upon)

जानकारी *f*   knowledge, information

जानना   to know

जाना-माना   well known, renowned

ज़ायका *m* a taste, a flavour

ज़ायकेदार tasty, delicious

जारी progressing, continuing

ज़ाहिर evident, apparent

ज़िक्र *m* a mention

जिठानी/जेठानी *f* a sister-in-law (wife of husband's elder brother)

जिज्ञासा *f* a desire to know, curiosity

ज़िम्मा *m* responsibility

ज़िम्मेदारी *f* a responsibility

जी expression of 1. respect/affection (used after names) 2. assent 3. enquiry

जी *m* spirits, bodily state

जी मचलाना/मतलाना to feel nausea

जीजाजी *m* a brother-in-law (elder sister's husband)

जीत *f* victory, a win

जीतना to win

जीते रहो may you have a long life!

जीभ *f* the tongue

ज़ीरा *m* cumin

जीवन *m* life

जीवाणु *m* bacteria

जुकाम *m* a cold

जुटना to be involved/absorbed

जूता *m* a shoe

जेठ *m* a brother-in-law (husband's elder brother)

जैसे ही as soon as

जोड़ा *m*/जोड़ी *f* a couple, a pair

जोड़ी बनना to make a good couple

ज़ोर *m* strength, force

ज़ोर से severely, violently

ज़ोर-शोर *m* with great enthusiasm

जोश *m* passion, enthusiasm

ज़्यादा 1. very many, much 2. more

ज़्यादा से ज़्यादा at most

ज़्यादातर most, most commonly

ज्योति *f* light, radiance

झ

झकझोर देना to shake violently, to jolt

ट

टमाटर *m* a tomato

टहलना to go for a walk, to stroll

टोकरी *f* a basket

ठ

ठंडा/ठंढा cold

ठीक 1. right, true 2. exact 3. well

ड

डर *m* fear

डर जाना to be frightened, get a fright

डाक *f* post, mail

डाक-ख़ाना/डाक-घर *m* a post office

समुद्री डाक *f* surface post

हवाई डाक *f* airmail

डाक्टर *m* a doctor

डालना 1. to put 2. to throw (down/in)

डिगरी/डिग्री *f* a degree

डिब्बा/डब्बा *m* 1. a railway carriage 2. a box, a carton

डूबना to sink, to set (the sun)

डेढ़ one and a half

ड्यूटी *f* duty

ड्राइवर *m* a driver

ढ

ढंग *m* a way, a manner, a method

ढाई/अढ़ाई two and a half

ढीला loose

ढूँढना to look for, to search (out)

ढेर a heap, a pile

ढेर-से many

त

तंग tight
तंग करना to pester, to badger, to trouble
तंदूर *m* a traditional clay oven
तक 1. until 2. up to, as far as
तकनीकी technical
तक़रीबन approximately, about
तकलीफ़ *f* trouble, difficulty, distress
तजुर्बा/तजुरबा *m* experience
तनख़्वाह *f*/तनख़्या *f*/वेतन *m* a salary, pay
तनाव *m* tension
तबादला *m* a transfer
तबीयत/तबियत *f* state of health
  तबीयत ख़राब होना to be/feel unwell
तमस् *f* darkness, ignorance
तमीज़ *f* courtesy, manners
तय करना to decide
तरकारी *f* green vegetables
तरक़्क़ी *f* a promotion, progress
तरफ़ *f* a side, a direction
तरह *f* 1. a kind, a type 2. a manner
  अच्छी तरह से well
  (की) तरह like, as, in the manner of
  तरह-तरह का of many kinds, various
तरीक़ा *m* a method, a way, a tactic
तलाश *f* a search
ताज़ा fresh
तारीख़ *f* a date
तारीफ़ *f* praise
तीव्र acute, strong, intense
तुच्छ worthless, contemptible
तुरंत quickly, at once
तू-तड़ाक *m* rudeness
  तू-तड़ाक करना to hurl abuse,
                 to squabble
तूफ़ान *m* a storm
तृप्ति *f* satisfaction
तेज़ 1. high (fever, etc.) 2. strong (sun,
  wind, etc.) 3. intelligent
तेजपत्ता *m* a bay-leaf

तेज़ी *f* speed
तेल *m* oil
तैयार ready, prepared
  तैयारी *f* readiness, preparation(s)
तौर *m* a manner, a way
तौलना to weigh
त्यागना to give up
त्याग-पत्र *m* a letter of resignation
त्योहार *m* a festival
त्वचा *f* the skin

थ

थकना to be tired
थान *m* a piece, a bolt/ a roll (of cloth)
थैली *f* a small bag, a sachet
थोड़ा a little, few, a few
  थोड़े ही hardly, by no means

द

दक्षिण south, southern
दफ़ा हो जाओ! Get lost! Beat it!
दफ़्तर *m* an office, a workplace
दबाना to press
दम *m* strength, vigour, mettle
दरवाज़ा *m* a door a doorway
दरी *f* a cotton rug, a carpet
दर्जन *m* a dozen
दर्ज़ी *m* a tailor
दर्द *m* pain
दर्शक *m* a viewer
दर्शनीय worth seeing, picturesque
दल *m* a (political) party, a group
दलित trampled, oppressed
दलित *m* a Dalit. Self-designation for a
            group of people traditionally
            regarded as low-caste or
            untouchables
दवा *f* a medicine
दस्त *m* diarrhoea, dysentery
दही *m* yoghurt

दाख़िला *m* admission

दाग़ *m* a spot, a stain

दाद *f* praise, appreciation

दादा *m* a paternal grandfather

दादी *f* a paternal grandmother

दाम *m* a price, a rate, cost

दाल *f* lentils, cooked lentils

   दाल मक्खनी *f* black lentils cooked in a rich spicy sauce

दाहिना right (hand)

   दाहिनी ओर right hand, on/to the right

दिखना/दिखाई देना to be visible, to appear

दिखाना to show

दिन *m* a day, daytime

दिल *m* the heart

   दिल का डाक्टर a cardiologist

   दिल का रोग heart disease

   दिल बहलाना *m* to distract, to divert the mind from cares

दिलचस्पी *f* an interest

दिशा *f* a direction

दीदी/जीजी *f* an elder sister

दीप/दीपक/दीया *m* a lamp, a light

दीपावली/दीवाली *f* Diwali

दीवाना fanatical, mad

   दीवानापन *m* madness, a frenzy

दुकान *m* a shop

दुनिया *f*/विश्व *m* the world

दुबारा repeated, a second time

दुर्गा *f* the goddess Durga

दुर्घटना *f* an accident

दुर्दशा *f* a sad plight, misery

दूना twice as much

दूर far away, distant

दूरी *f* a distance

दूरदर्शन *m* television

दूसरा second, next, other

देखना to see, to inspect

   देखने लायक worth seeing

देना to give

देर से late

देरी *f* a delay, lateness

देव-स्थान *m* a place of worship

देवता *m* a god

देवी *f* 1. a goddess 2. a lady

देश *m* a country

   देशी national, indigenous, internal

   देश प्रेम *m* patriotism

देहांत *m* death

दैनिक daily, *also m* daily newspaper

दोनों the two, both

दौरा *m* a fit, an attack (of illness, etc.)

ध

धड़ाम *m* any sudden loud sound, thud

   धड़ाम से with a thud, crash, etc.

धन *m* money, riches, wealth

   धन-दौलत *f* wealth and riches

धनिया *f/m* coriander

   हरी धनिया *f* fresh coriander leaves

धन्यवाद thank you

धमाका *m* a loud noise, blast, explosion

धर्म *m* religion

धीमा 1. low, weak 2. slow, sluggish

धीरे-धीरे slowly, softly, quietly

धूप *f* sunshine, the heat of the sun

धूप *m*/धूपबत्ती *f* incense

धूम-धाम *f* display, ostentation

न

नंबर *m* मिलाना to dial a phone number

न/ना? 1. not 2. *rhetorical* is it not so?

नक़्क़ाशी *f* carving

नज़दीक near, close

नज़दीकी *f* proximity *adj.* near, close

नज़र *f* sight, a glance

   नज़र आना to come into view

नदारद absent/gone, lost

नमक *m* salt

नमकीन *m* salted food, a savoury snack

नमस्ते greetings! A common spoken greeting or word of farewell

नया new

नवयुवक *m, pl* youth

नाक *f* the nose

नाक बहना *nose*: to run

नागपुर Nagpur (a city in the state of Maharashtra)

नागरिक *m* a citizen

नाच *m* dance, dancing

नाचना to dance, to caper

नाटक *m* a drama, a play

नाड़ी *f* the pulse

नान *f* a leavened flatbread baked in a clay oven

नाना *m* a maternal grandfather

नानी *f* a maternal grandmother

नाप *f* size, measure

नापना to measure (out)

अपना रास्ता नापो Go away! Make yourself scarce!

नाम होना to have a name/reputation

नालायक incapable, unworthy

नाश्ता *m* breakfast; a light snack

नाहक़ needlessly, without good cause

निकालना to get rid of

नियत fixed, appointed, arranged

निर्णय *m* a decision, a judgement

निर्णय लेना/करना to decide

निर्देशक *m* a director

निर्भर dependent

निश्चय *m* a decision, a resolve

निश्चिंत free from worry, unperturbed

निहायत extremely, exceedingly

नींद *f* sleep

नीच base, mean

नीचे below, under, underneath

नीला blue

नुक़सान *m* harm, damage

नुक़सान पहुँचाना/करना to do damage, to harm, to destroy

नुसख़ा *m* a prescription

नृत्य *m* dance

नेक good, excellent, worthy

नेता *m* a leader, a politician

नैवेद्य *m* an offering, food consecrated to a deity

नौकर *m* a servant, attendant

नौकरी *f* work, employment

प

पंखा *m* a fan

पंखा करना to fan

पकना to be cooked

पकवान *m* a delicacy; cooked food

पक्का definite(ly), sure(ly), fixed

पछताना to repent, to regret

पटाका *m* a firecracker

पड़ना 1. to have to
2. to occur, to take place
3. to be found, located
4. to be put (in), added (to)

पड़ोसी *m* a neighbour

पढ़ना 1. to study 2. to read

पढ़ाई *f* study

पढ़ाना to teach

पतला thin

पता *m* 1. an address 2. information

पता करना/लगाना to find out

पता होना *m* to know

पति *m* a husband

पतीला *m* a wide mouthed pot or pan

पत्ता *m*/पत्ती *f* 1. a strip 2. a leaf

पत्नी *f* a wife

पत्र *m* a letter

पत्रिका *f* a magazine, a journal

पद *m* a post, a position

पदार्थ *m* 1. a product 2. a substance
पनीर *m* a firm fresh cheese made with curdled milk
पन्ना *m* a page
परंपरा *f* tradition
 परंपरागत traditional
परखना to judge, to test
परची *f*/परचा *m* label, a piece of paper
परदेशी *m* a foreigner
परवाह/परवा *f* care, concern
 (की) परवाह करना to care (about)
परसना/परोसना to serve food
पराजय *f*/हार *f* defeat
पराठा/पराँठा *m* a fried flaky multi-layered flatbread
परामर्श *m* advice, consultation
परिणाम *m* a result
परियोजना *f* a project
परिवर्तन *m* a change, a transformation
परिवार *m* a family
परीक्षा *f* an examination
परेशान worried, distressed
पर्व *m* a festival, a holiday
पल *m* a moment, an instant
पवित्र pure, sacred
पश्मीना *m* pashmina, fine cashmere
पसंद आना to please, to be liked (by)
पसंद करना to like, to choose
पसंद होना to please, to be liked (by)
पहचानना to recognise
पहनना to put on (clothes), to wear
पहला first, previous
पहले 1. first 2. earlier, previously
 (स) पहले before, earlier than
पहुँचना to arrive, to reach
पहुँचाना 1. to escort 2. to deliver
पहेली *f* a riddle
 पहेलियाँ बुझाना to speak in riddles
पाउच *m* a small bag, a sachet
पाउडर *m* powder

पाक *m* a dish, something cooked
पाजामा *m* loose cotton trousers
पाठ्यक्रम *m* a course, a programme
पाठ्यचर्या *m* a syllabus, a curriculum
पानी *m* water
 पानी की कमी *f* dehydration
पाबंदी *f* due observance
पार्क *m* a park
पालक *m* spinach
पालन *m* observing, complying
पालन करना to observe, to comply with
पाव *m* a quarter
पास 1. near 2. with, on, owned by
पिक्चर *f* a film
पिता *m* a father
पिलाना to give to drink
पिसता *m* a pistachio nut
पी.एच.डी. *m* PhD, a doctorate
पीछा छोड़ना to leave alone
पीछे behind, at the back
पीना to drink
पीला yellow
 पीला-सा yellowish
पुकारना to call out
पुजारी *m* the priest of a temple
पुणे *m* Pune, a city in the state of Maharashtra
पुताई *f* whitewashing
पुरातत्व *m* archaeology
पुराना old, of long standing
पुरुष *m* a man
पुलाव *m* pilau/pilaf: a spiced rice dish with vegetables or meat
पुस्तक *f* a book
पूछ-ताछ *f* an enquiry
पूछना to ask, to enquire of
पूजना to worship
पूजा *f* worship, a religious ceremony
पूरा whole, complete
 पूरा आना to fit

पूर्ण   whole, full

पूर्ण बहुमत *f*   an absolute majority

पूर्ति *f*   the satisfaction of a need/a want

पेट *m*   the stomach

पेट ख़राब होना   to have an upset
stomach

पेटी *f*   a box, a case

पेड़ *m*   a tree

पेशा *m*   an occupation, a profession

पैक करना   to pack

पैकेट/पैकिट *m*   a packet, a parcel

पैदा करना   to create, to produce

पैर रखने की जगह न होना   to be crowded

पैसा *m*   1. money 2. a coin equal in
value to 1/100th of a rupee

पोता *m*   a grandson (son's son)

पोती *f*   a granddaughter
(son's daughter)

पोस्टकार्ड *m*   a postcard

प्याज़ *m*   an onion

प्रकार *m*   a kind, a sort, a type

प्रणाम *m*   a respectful greeting

प्रतिमा *f*   an image, a likeness, an idol

प्रतियोगिता *f*   a competition

प्रतिशत *f*   per cent

प्रतिष्ठान *m*   a foundation, an institute

प्रतीक *m*   a symbol

प्रतीक्षा *f*   a wait

प्रथा *f*   a tradition, a custom

प्रथानुसार   according to custom

प्रदूषण *m*   (environmental) pollution

प्रधान मंत्री *m*   a prime minister

प्रबंध *m*   organisation, management

प्रबंधक *m*   a manager

प्रबंधन संस्थान *m*   a business school

प्रभावित   influenced, impressed

प्रवेश *m*   an entry, an admission

प्रवेश करना   to enter

प्रवेश-परीक्षा *f*   an entrance exam

प्रशिक्षण *m*   training

प्रसन्न   pleased, delighted

प्रसाद *m*   a devotional offering made to
a god, typically food later
shared among devotees

प्रांत *m*   a region, a province, a state

प्राध्यापक *m*   a (university) lecturer

प्राप्त करना   to obtain

प्रेम कथा *f*   a love story

प्रेम कहानी *f*   a love story

प्रोत्साहन *m*   encouragement

प्रौढ़ शिक्षा *f*   adult education

फ्लैटफ़ॉर्म *m*   a (railway) platform

फ

फटना   to burst

फ़र्क/फ़रक *m*   a difference

फ़र्क/फ़रक   different, distinct

फल *m*   1. fruit 2. a return, a reward

फलवाला *f*   a fruit seller/vendor

फल मिलना   to obtain the fruits/results

फ़ायदा *m*   an advantage, a benefit

फ़ार्म *m*   a form

फ़ालतू   surplus, spare

फ़िक्र/फ़िकर *f*   concern, anxiety

फिर   1. again 2. afterwards, then, next

फिर कभी   some other time

फिर मिलेंगे   see you later

फ़िलहाल   at the present time, for the
time being

फ़िल्म *f*   a film

फ़ुरसत/फ़ुर्सत *f*   leisure, free time

फूफा *m*   an uncle (father's sister's
husband)

फुलझड़ी *f*   a sparkler

फेफड़ा *m*   the lung

फैलना   to spread

फ़ैसला *m*/निर्णय *m*/निश्चय *m*   a decision

फ़ोटो *f*   a photograph

फ़ोन करना   to ring up

फ़ौरन   immediately

फ़्रिज *m*   a fridge

फ़्लैट *m*   a flat

    फ़्लैट लेना   to buy/rent a flat

ब

बक्श़ाना   to spare

बग़ल (में)   adjoining, nearby

बग़ीचा / बाग़ीचा *m*   a garden

बचना   to be saved, to escape

बचपन *m*   childhood

बच्ची *f*   a little girl, a baby girl

बजाना   to play (a musical instrument)

बड़ा   1. big 2. senior in years, elder
      3. very, exceedingly

बड़बड़ाना   to mutter, to grumble

बढ़ना   to increase, to grow

बढ़िया   excellent, fine

बताना   1. to inform, to tell, to describe
      2. to explain, to show

बत्ती *f*   a light, a lamp

बदतमीज़   rude, ill-mannered

बदतर   worse

बदबू *f*   a bad smell, a stench

    बदबूदार   stinking, smelling

बदलना   1. to change, to be transformed
      2. to exchange

बदली *f*   a transfer

बदले में   in place of, in exchange for

बधाई *f*   congratulation(s)

बनना   to be made/prepared

बनाना   to make, to prepare (food, etc.)

    बना-बनाया   ready-made

बम *m*   a bomb

बम्बई *f*   Bombay/Mumbai

    बम्बई सेंट्रल *m*   Bombay Central
        railway station

बरफ़ी / बर्फ़ी *f*   a rectangular sweet made
        from crushed nuts or
        thickened milk and sugar

(के) बराबर   comparable to, equal

बर्थ *f*   a berth on a train

बल-बूता *m*   power, strength, might

बलग़म *m*   phlegm, mucus

बला *f*   an awful/terrible person/thing

बल्कि   but rather

बस *f*   a bus

बस   1. enough 2. only, merely

बहनजी *f*   a sister, a polite form of
        address for a woman

बहना   to flow

बहस *f*   an argument/a dispute/a quarrel

बहाना *m*   an excuse, a pretext

बहुजन समाज पार्टी / बसपा *f*   a national
        political party

बहुत   1. enough 2. ample 3. very

बहुमत *f*   a majority

बहुराष्ट्रीय   multinational

बहू *f*   a daughter-in-law

बाँटना   to distribute, to share

बांधना   to pack

बाएँ   to the left

बाक़ी   remaining

    बाकी होना   to be left, to remain

बाज़ार *m*   a market

बात *f*   a matter, a concern, a thing

    बात पक्की होना   to be a settled matter

    बात बनाना   to invent a story

बाद   afterwards

    (के) बाद   after

बादाम *m*   an almond

बाप रे बाप!   *interjection* good heavens!

बापू *m*   a father (*also:* 'father of the
        nation', used for M.K. Gandhi)

बायीं तरफ़   (on the) left side

बार-बार   again and again, repeatedly

बारी *f*   a time, a turn

बारीक   fine, thin

(के) बारे में   about, concerning

बॉलीवुड   Bollywood (collective term
        for commercial Hindi cinema)

बाहर 1. out, outside 2. away, abroad

बिकना to be sold

 बिक चुकना to be sold (out)

बिगड़ना to deteriorate, to be spoiled

बिगाड़ना to spoil, to ruin

बिछना to be spread out

बिल *m* a bill, an account

बिलकुल entirely, completely

 बिलकुल नहीं not at all, no way

बिस्तर *m* a bed, bedclothes

बी.ए. *m* a bachelor's degree

बीतना *time* to pass, to elapse

बीमार पड़ना to fall ill

बीवी *f* a wife

बुआ / फूफ़ी *f* an aunt (father's sister)

बुक करना to reserve, to book

बुकिंग *f* a reservation, a booking

बुख़ार *m* a fever

बुद्धि *f* intelligence, the mind

बुद्धिजीवी intellectual

बुधवार *m* Wednesday

बुरा bad

 (किसी का) बुरा हाल करना to reduce
   (*someone*) to a sad state

बुलाना to call, to send for, to invite

बूता *m* power, strength, might

 (के) बूते पर on the strength of

बेचनेवाली *f* a saleswoman

बेचारा *m* a wretch, a helpless person

बेटा *m* 1. a son 2. a form of address
   used by adults for children

बेशक undoubtedly, certainly

बेहद boundless, immense(ly)

बेहोश होना to faint, to have a blackout

बेहोशी *f* unconsciousness, a blackout

बेसन *m* gram/ chickpea flour

बैक्टीरियल bacterial

बैठाना / बिठाना to give a seat, to seat

बैरा *m* a waiter

बोनस *m* a bonus

बोलना to speak, to talk

बांकाइटिस *f* bronchitis

ब्लॉक *m* a block (of flats, etc.)

भ

भगवान् *m* a venerated deity, a god

भगाना to chase away

भजन *m* a devotional song, a hymn

 भजन-कीर्तन *m* singing and praising

भतीजा *m* a nephew (brother's son)

भतीजी *f* a niece (brother's daughter)

भयानक terrible

भरती *f* admission, enrolment

भरना to fill, to be full

 पेट भरना to be sated/satiated/stuffed

भरवाँ *food* stuffed

भरा full

भरोसा *m* confidence, faith, hope

 भरोसा दिलाना to assure

भला indeed, in truth

भलामानस *m* a good man, a courteous
        person; *ironic* a simpleton

भवन *m* a home, an abode; a building

भाग *m* a part

भाग-दौड़ *f* hectic activity

भागना to run away, to flee, to avoid

भाग्यशाली lucky, fortunate

भानजा / भांजा *m* a nephew (sister's son)

भानजी / भांजी *f* a niece (sister's daughter)

भाभी *m* a sister-in-law (brother's wife)

भारत *m* India

 भारत का / की / के from India

 भारत-विद्या *f* Indology, Indian studies

भारतीय Indian

भारी 1. heavy 2. vast, crowded

भावना *f* a feeling, an emotion

भाषा *f* a language

भिंडी *f* okra (a green vegetable)

भिगोना to wet, to soak, to steep

भीड़ *f* a crowd, a crush

भीड़-भाड़ *m* hustle and bustle, crowds

भुलाना to erase from the mind, to forget

(किसी का) भूत सवार होना to be possessed by a fiend, to be obsessed (*by something*)

भूनना to roast, to fry

भूलना to forget

भेजना to send

भैया *m* an (elder) brother

म

मंगवाना to order, to send for

मंज़िल *f* a storey, a floor

मंज़ूर accepted, agreeable, approved of

मंदिर *m* a temple

मक़बरा *m* a tomb, a mausoleum

मक़सद *m* aim, purpose, intention

मकान *m* a flat, a house, a dwelling

मक्खन *m* butter

मगर but

मचना to be caused, to be produced

मच्छर *m* a mosquito

मज़ा *m* pleasure, enjoyment, fun

मज़ा आना to have fun, to have a good time

मज़े में well, contented

मज़े में हूँ things are fine with me

मज़ेदार 1. interesting, amusing 2. *food* tasty, delicious

मज़ाक *m* a joke

मजाल *f* nerve, courage

तुम्हारी यह मजाल! How dare you!

मत *m* a vote

मतदान *m* voting, to vote

मतलब *m* 1. meaning 2. sense, point 3. an intention, a purpose

मतली *f* nausea

मदद *f* help, aid, support

मध्यम medium, moderate

मन *m* the mind, the heart, the soul

मन मोहना to captivate, to charm

(में) मन लगना to like, be pleased (by)

(में) मन लगाना to devote oneself (to)

मनपसंद liked, preferred

मना होना prohibited, not permitted

मनाना to celebrate

मनोरंजन *m* entertainment, amusement

मनोविज्ञान *m* psychology

मरम्मत *f* repair

मरम्मत करना *figurative* to give a good beating

मशहूर famous

मसाला *m* spices, a spice

मस्जिद *m* a mosque

महँगा expensive

महक *f* fragrance, an aroma

महत्व *m* importance

महल *m* a palace, a mansion

महसूस होना to be felt

महाराष्ट्र *m* Maharashtra (an Indian state)

महालक्ष्मी/लक्ष्मी *f* Lakshmi, the goddess of good fortune and wealth

महिला *f* a woman

महीन 1. fine 2. thin

माँग *f* a demand

माँस-मछली *f* meat and fish

माक्स म्युलर भवन *m* Max Mueller Bhawan (Name of the Goethe-Institut in India)

माध्यम *m* a medium

मानना 1. to agree 2. to believe

माना जाना to be considered

माने *m* a meaning

माफ़ कीजिये excuse me!

मामला *m* a matter, a concern

मामा *m* a maternal uncle

मामी *f* an aunt (maternal uncle's wife)

मामूली ordinary

मायका *m* mother's house, parental home (of a married woman)

मार-धाड़ *f* fighting, violence

मारे जाना to be killed

मार्ग *m* a road

माल *m* wares, goods

मालूम होना to be or become known

मासिक monthly

माहिर *m* an expert

(में) माहिर होना to be expert (in/at)

माहौल *m* an environment, a mood

मिट्टी *f* clay

मिठाई *f* a sweet

मिनट *m* a minute

मिर्च *f* a chilli; chilli powder

मिलना 1. to be found
2. to meet
3. to be available

मिलनसार sociable, friendly, affable

मिला-जुला mixed, assorted

मिलता-जुलता similar

मिश्रण *m* a mixture

मीटर *m* 1. a metre (unit of length)
2. a taxicab meter

मीटिंग *f* a meeting

मीठा sweet

मील *f* a mile

मुँह *m* 1. the face 2. the mouth

मुँह मीठा करना to give sweets (in celebration of a happy event)

मुख्य main, principal

मुख्यमंत्री *m* a chief minister

मुड़ना to turn

(के) मुताबिक according (to)

मुद्दा *m* an issue, a matter

मुफ्त free, gratis

मुर्ग *m* chicken

मुर्ग टिक्का *m* skewered chunks of chicken grilled in a clay oven

मुलायम soft

मुश्किल *f* a difficulty

मुसलमान *m* a Muslim

मुसीबत *f* trouble

मुहल्ला/मोहल्ला *m* a neighbourhood, a quarter (of a town)

मुहावरा *m* an idiom, an expression

मूर्ति-कला *f* sculpture

मूल 1. original 2.basic, fundamental

मेनू *m* a menu

मेमसाहब *f* *form of address* madam, lady

मेल बैठना to be compatible, harmonise

मेला *m* a fair, a market held regularly at a fixed place

मेवा *m* dried fruit, nuts

मेहनत *f* hard work, toil, industry

मेहमान *m* a guest

मेहरबानी *f* kindness

मैच *m* a sports match

मैदान *m* an open area, a playing field

मोमबत्ती *f* a candle

मोल-भाव *m* bargaining, haggling

मौका *m* a chance, an opportunity

मौसा *m* an uncle (maternal aunt's husband)

मौसी *f* a maternal aunt

य

(को) याद होना to be remembered/ recollected (by)

यानी/याने that is, i.e.

योग्य qualified, capable

योग्यता *f* qualification(s), ability

र

रंग *m* a colour

रंग-बिरंगा multicoloured

रंगीन coloured, colourful

रंगोली *f* a painted or floral decoration on a house wall or floor

रक्त *m* blood

रक्त दबाव *m* blood pressure

रखना to keep, to put aside

रट *f* repetition

  रट लगाना to repeat ad nauseam

रतनागिरी *m* Ratnagiri (a town in the
                  state of Maharashtra)

रवाना होना to depart

रविवार *m* Sunday

रसगुल्ला *m* a sweet spongy ball of
                 soft cheese soaked in syrup

रसभरा juicy

रसेदार/शोरबेदार cooked in a sauce or
                 gravy

रसोई *f* 1. a kitchen 2. food

रस्म *f* a custom, a ceremony

राजनीति *f* politics

रात *f* a night; nighttime

  रात का खाना *m* dinner

  रात-दिन night and day

  रात-दिन एक करना work night and day

  रात भर the whole night

रामचंदजी *m* the god Ram(a), hero of
             the epic poem *Ramayana*

राय *f* advice, opinion

रायता *m* a side dish of finely chopped
          vegetables or fruit in yoghurt

राष्ट्र *m* a nation, a country

राष्ट्रीय national

रास्ता *m* a way

राह-चलता *m* a passerby

राहत *f* relief

रिक्शेवाला *m* a rickshaw driver

रिवाज *m* a custom, a practice

रिश्ता *m* a relationship, an alliance

  रिश्ता आना to receive a proposal of
            marriage

  रिश्तेदार *m, pl* a relative

रुकना to stop

रुचि *f* an interest, a liking

रुझान *m* a tendency, an inclination

रुपया *m* a rupee

रूढ़िवादी conservative, traditional

रूप *m* a manner, a form

रेलवे स्टेशन *m* a railway station

रेस्तराँ/रेस्तोराँ/रेस्टोरेंट *m* a restaurant

रेशम *m* silk

रोकना 1. to stop, halt 2. to obstruct

रोग *m* an illness, a disease

रोज़मर्रा *m* daily, the daily life

रोटी *f* a round unleavened flatbread

रोशनी *f* light

रौनक़ *f* an atmosphere of excitement

ल

लंबा long

लक्षण *m* a symptom

लक्ष्मी/महालक्ष्मी *f* Lakshmi, the goddess
            of good fortune and wealth

लक्ष्मीनारायण *m* the depiction of the
           Hindu god Vishnu with
           his consort Lakshmi

लगना 1. to be felt, experienced
      2. to cost 3. *cooking* to be burnt

लगभग approximately

लगाव *m* attachment, affection

लघु-चित्र *m* a miniature (painting)

लज़ीज़ delicious, delightful

लड़का *m* a boy

लड़की *f* 1. a girl 2. a daughter
         3. future wife

लड़ना 1. to collide 2. to fight, quarrel

लड़ाई *f* an altercation, a fight, a quarrel

लड्डू *m* a ball of thickened milk or
         flour, etc. with sugar

लवण *m* salt(s)

लहसुन *m* garlic

लाइन *f* 1. a telephone connection/line;
      2. a railway line

लाड़-प्यार *m* love and affection

लाभ *m* a benefit, an advantage

  लाभ उठाना to take advantage, profit

लिटर a litre

लिहाज़ *m* consideration, respect

लेकिन but

लेख *m* an article, an essay

लेखा-जेखा *m* an account, a reckoning, an assessment

  लेखा-जेखा करना to reassess, to take stock

लेटना to lie down

लेना to take

  लेना-देना *m* a connection, a relation

लेप *m* an ointment, a paste

लोकतंत्र *m* a democracy

लोकप्रिय popular

लोकल ट्रेन *f* a local/commuter train

लोकोक्ति *f* a proverb

लोग *pl, m* people

लोशन *m* a lotion

लौंग *m* a clove

व

व and

वंचित deprived

वक़्त *m* time

  वक़्त/समय की पाबंदी *f* punctuality

वग़ैरा/वग़ैरह and so forth, et cetera

वज़न *m* weight

वजह *f* a cause, a reason

वनवास *m* exile, banishment to a forest

वर्ग *m* a social group, a class

वर्ष *m* a year

वसूल करना to collect

वस्तु *f* a thing, an article

वस्त्र *m* clothes

वाकई real(ly), truly

वातावरण *m* an environment, a mood

वाद्य *m* a musical instrument

वापस back

वारदात *f* an incident, a disaster

वार्षिक annual

वास्तव *m* में in reality, actually

विक्रेता *m* a salesman, a trader

विचार *m* 1. an opinion, a viewpoint
        2. a thought, an idea
        3. reflection, consideration

विजयी victorious

विज्ञान *m* science

विज्ञापान *m* an advertisement

विदेश *m* a foreign country

विदेशी foreign

विद्यार्थी *m, pl* a student

विधानसभा *f* the Legislative Assembly

विभाग *m* a department

विशाल huge

विश्व *m* the world

  विश्वकप *m* the world championship

  विश्वविद्यालय *m* a university

विश्वास *m* faith, belief

विषय *m* a subject, a topic

विष्णु *m* Vishnu, one of the three main Hindu gods, seen as the preserver of the universe

विस्फोट *m* an explosion

वैसे तो on the whole, in fact

वोट *m* a vote

व्यंजन *m* a dish

व्यवस्था *f* an arrangement, measures

व्यस्त occupied, busy

व्यापारी *m* a merchant, a trader

व्यावसायिक professional, occupational

श

शक *m* a suspicion

शक्ति *f* power, strength

शख्स *m* a person, an individual

शग़ल *m* a pastime, an occupation

  (से) शग़ल करना to pass time, to occupy oneself (with)

शनिवार *m* Saturday

शपथ *f* an oath

शपथ लेना to take an oath

शब्द-कोश *m* a dictionary

शरीफ़ noble, wellborn, refined

शरीर *m* the body

शर्त *f* a condition, terms

शर्माना/शरमाना to be embarrassed

शर्मिंदा/शरमिंदा होना to be embarrassed

शलवार *m* loose pleated trousers with a
      drawstring waist

   शलवार-कमीज़ *f* a suit consisting of
         loose trousers com-
         bined with a tunic

शहद *m* honey

शहर *m* a city, a town

शांत quiet, tranquil, peaceful

शांति *f* peace, tranquillity

शाकाहारी vegetarian

शाख़ा *f* a branch

शादी *f* marriage, a wedding

   शादी करवाना to get someone married

शानदार magnificent

शाबाश Well done! Splendid!

शाम *f* the evening

शामिल included

शायद perhaps, maybe

शॉल *m* a shawl

शास्त्रीय संगीत *m* classical music

शिकायत *f* a complaint

शिक्षण *m* teaching, instruction

शिक्षा *f* education

शिमला-मिर्च *f* a pepper/capsicum

शिव *m* Shiv(a), one of the three
      main Hindu gods, seen as
      both the destroyer and the
      creator of the universe

शीरा *f* a sugar syrup

शुक्र *m* 1. gratitude 2. thanksgiving

   शुक्र है कि thank god/heavens for...!

शुक्रिया *m* thank you

शुभ auspicious

शुभाशीष *m* a blessing

शुरू करना to begin, to start

शुल्क *m* a fee (as for entrance)

शोध-कार्य *m* research work

शोर-गुल *m* noise, a din, hubbub

शोरबेदार cooked in a sauce/gravy

शौक़ *m* an interest, pleasure, eagerness

   शौक़ से gladly, with pleasure

शौक़ीन *m/adj* a connoisseur, a buff;
         fond, keen

श्रीखंड *m* a creamy yoghurt dessert

श्रीमती *f* Mrs. (form of address for
         married women)

श्रेष्ठ best, most excellent

स

संकलन *m* a collection

संकाय *m* a faculty

संक्रमण *m* an infection

संख्या *f* a number

संगठन *m* an organisation

संगीत *m* music

   संगीत प्रेमी *m* a music lover

संग्रहालय *m* a museum

संचालन *m* management

संदूषित contaminated

संध्या *f* the evening

संपत्ति *f* wealth, riches, prosperity

संपदा *f* an abundance

संपर्क *m* contact, liaison, relationship

   संपर्क अधिकारी *m* PR Manager, liaison
         officer

संबंध *m* a connection, a relationship

   संबंध बनाना to establish a link, to
         forge a relationship

संबंधित connected, related

संबंधी *m, adj* 1. a relative 2. related

संबोधित करना to address

संभालना 1. to take care of 2. to support
 संभाल कर with care, carefully
संयुक्त joint
संयोग *m* a coincidence
संस्कृत *f* the Sanskrit language
संस्कृति *f* culture
संस्थान *m* /संस्था *f* an institute,
                       an organisation
सकना to be able
सगा born of the same parents
सचमुच really, truly
सजना to dress up, to be adorned
सजाना to arrange, to decorate
सजावट *f* arrangement, decoration
सज्जा *f* decoration
सड़क *f* a road
सतर्क alert, watchful
सताना to torment, to torture
सत्ता *m* power, authority (political or
         administrative)
सदस्य *m* a member
सनसनीख़ेज़ sensational
सन्नाटा *m* a dead silence, stillness
सफ़र *m* a journey; travelling
सफलता *f* success
सफ़ाई *f* 1. cleanliness 2. cleaning
सफ़ेद *m* white
सब्ज़ी *f* a vegetable; a vegetable dish
समझदार intelligent, discerning
समझना 1. to understand
        2. to consider, to perceive
समझ-बूझकर prudently
समझाना 1. to explain 2. to admonish
समय *m* time
समर्थन *m* support
समस्या *f* a problem
समाचार *m* the news
 समाचार पत्र *m* a newspaper
समाज *m* society
 समाज सेवा *f* social work

समाधान *m* a solution (of a problem)
समूह *m* a collection, a group
समोसा *m* a fried triangular-shaped
           pasty with a savoury filling
सरकार *f* the government
 सरकारी governmental, official
सवा plus a quarter
सवारी *f* 1. a ride 2. conveyance
सर्वेक्षण *m* a survey
सवाल *m* a question, an issue
 सवाल-जवाब *m* a discussion, a debate
ससुर *m* a father-in-law
 ससुराल *m* father-in-law's house
सहकर्ता *m* a colleague
सहकर्मी *m* a colleague
सहमत होना to agree
सहमना to feel fear
सहयोग *m* support, cooperation
सहायता *f* help, assistance, aid
सहित along with, together with
सही quite right, correct, exactly
सहेली *f* a woman's female friend
साँस *f* a breath
 साँस लेना to breathe, to draw breath
सांस्कृतिक cultural
साइकिल *f* a bicycle
साक्षरता *f* literacy
साढ़े plus a half
 साढ़े सात (बजे) half past seven
साथ *m* 1. company 2. a close bond
सादा plain, unadorned, simple
साधन *m* means
साफ़ 1. clean
      2. plain, clear
साबित proved, confirmed
सामग्री *f* materials, ingredients
सामने in front, facing
सामान *m* 1. luggage
           2. goods, things, provisions
सारा all, whole, entire

सार्थक *m*   meaningful, significant

सास *f*   a mother-in-law

साहित्य *m*   literature

सिंक *m*   a washbasin

सिखाना   to teach, to instruct

सितारवादन *m*   sitar playing

सितारा *m*   a star, a filmstar

सिद्धांत *m*   a principle

सिनेमा *m*   1. cinema 2. a film

   सिनेमा-घर *m*   a cinema, a movie
                  theatre

सिर / सर *m*   the head

   सिर खाना   to get on someone's nerves

   सिर-दर्द *m*   a headache

सिर्फ़   only, merely

सिलवाना   to have sewn (by someone)

सिलसिलेवार   linked, serial, sequential

(के) सिवा   except, apart from

सीखना   to learn

सीट *f*   a seat

सीधा   1. straight, direct
        2. right (hand)

   सीधा-सादा   plain, unadorned, simple

   सीधे जाना   to go straight (ahead)

सुंदर   beautiful

सुख *m*   happiness, joy

सुगंध *f*   fragrance, a sweet smell

   सुगंधित / ख़ुश्बूदार   perfumed, fragrant

सुझाव *m*   a suggestion

सुधरना   to improve

सुधार *m*   an improvement

सुबह *f*   the morning; in the morning

सुरक्षा *f*   security, safety

सुराग *m*   a sign, a trace, a clue

सुर्ख़ी *f*   a headline

सुविधा *f*   a facility, a convenience,
            a service

सुशील   of good character or disposition

सूखा   dry

सूचना-पट्ट *m*   a signboard

सूचना प्रौद्योगिकी *f*   IT, information
                   technology

सूचित करना   to inform

सूची *f*   a list

सूती   made of cotton

सूरज *m*   the sun

सेब *m*   an apple

सेवा *f*   service

सैर *f*   1. a walk, a stroll 2. an outing,
        a tour

सोचना   to think, to reflect

   सोच-विचार *m*   careful consideration

सौंपना   to entrust, to hand over

स्तर *m*   a level, a grade

स्थल *m*   a place

स्थान *m*   1. a place, a spot
            2. a position, a rank

स्थापना *f*   establishment, founding

   स्थापित   placed, fixed

स्थिति *f*   1. a position 2. a situation

स्नातक स्तर *m*   a bachelor's degree

स्नातकोत्तर   postgraduate

स्पष्ट   clear

स्मारक *m*   a memorial, a monument

स्वयं सेवी   volunteer

स्वस्थ   healthy

   स्वस्थ हो जाना   to recover, to get well

स्वागत *m*   a welcome; a reception

स्वादिष्ट   tasty, delicious

स्वास्थ्य *m*   health

ह

हँसमुख   cheerful

हँसी-मज़ाक *f*   laughing and joking,
                 joviality

हकीकत *f*   reality, the truth, fact

हज़ार *m*   a thousand

हटाना   to remove, to move away/aside

हत्या *m*   a killing, a murder

हत्यारा *m*   a murderer

हनुमान *m* the chief of the monkeys in the epic *Ramayana*, worshipped by Hindus as a god

हफ़्ता *m* a week

हमला *m* an attack

हमलावार *m* anattacker

हमेशा always

हरा green

हर्ज *m* harm, loss, damage

हल *m* a solution (of a problem)

हलका light, pale (*colour*)

हलवाई *m* a sweet-maker, a sweet-seller

हल्दी *f* turmeric

हस्तशिल्प *m* a handicraft

हस्ताक्षर *m* a signature

हाज़िरी *f* बजाना to report on duty

हाथ *m* the hand

हाथ के हाथ on-the-spot, directly

हाथ धो के पीछे पड़ना to pursue someone relentlessly, to hound

हाथ लगाना to touch

हादसा *m* an incident, an accident

हाफ़ुस, आल्फ़ौंज़ो *m* a variety of mango

हाय राम! *interjection* oh God!

हार *f* defeat

हार-जीत *f* defeat and victory, losing and winning

हारना to lose

हार्दिक cordial, hearty

हाल में recently

हाल-चाल *m* a state, a condition, a situation

हालत *f* a state (of affairs), a condition

हर हालत में in any case, at any rate

हालाँकि 1. although 2. however

हालात *f* a particular state, circumstances

हासिल करना to acquire, to get

हिट *m/f* a hit, a popular film, song, etc.

हिम्मत *f* spirit, courage

हिम्मत *f* हारना to become dispirited, to lose heart

हिल जाना to be shaken, agitated

हिसाब *m* 1. a price, a rate 2. accounts

हिसाब करना to calculate/total up an account

हिस्सा *m* a part

हीरो *m* a hero, a male lead (in a film)

हीरोइन *f* a heroine, a female lead (in a film)

हुज्जत *f* an argument, an objection (esp.frivolous)

हृदयरोग *m* heart disease

हैज़ा / कॉलेरा *m* cholera

हैरान amazed/perplexed

होटल *m* a hotel, *also* restaurant

होश *m* आना to recover consciousness

होशियार intelligent

Handwörterbuch Hindi-Deutsch

Hrsg. von Margot Gatzlaff-Hälsig. Unter Mitarbeit von Lutz Baganz, Barbara Börner-Westphal, Hannelore Bauhaus-Lötzke und Christina Oesterheld.
2002. XXVIII, 1.448 Seiten.
978-3-87548-177-8. Gebunden

Mit rund 50.000 Stichwörtern, zahlreichen Beispielen, Redewendungen und Sprichwörtern erfasst dieses vollständig neu erarbeitete Handwörterbuch den Wortschatz des Standard- oder Hochhindi und darüber hinaus geläufige Ausdrücke der Umgangssprache sowie lokale Varianten und Fachtermini verschiedener Gebiete.

Alle Stichwörter bis hin zu den Redewendungen sind mit grammatischen Angaben versehen. Besondere Beachtung finden abweichende Satzkonstruktionen und die Rektion der Verben. Jedem (in Devanagari-Schrift gegebenen) Stichwort folgt als Aussprachehilfe eine Transliteration.

Wörterbuch Deutsch–Hindi

Von Margot Gatzlaff-Hälsig.
6., unveränderte Auflage 2000.
646 Seiten. 978-3-87548-247-8.
Gebunden

Die rund 25.000 deutschen Stichwörter und Wendungen umfassen den Wortschatz der Alltagssprache sowie Termini aus dem gesellschaftlich-politischen Leben, den Geistes- und Naturwissenschaften, der Technik, der Wirtschaft und dem Sport. Darüber hinaus sind die wichtigsten geografischen Namen aufgeführt.

Alle Hindi-Äquivalente sind mit grammatischen Angaben versehen, die für eine richtige Satzbildung im Hindi unerlässlich sind.

Grammatische Angaben zum deutschen Stichwort, wie die Kennzeichnung der Tonsilbe, Aussprachehilfen, Deklinations- und Konjugationshinweise sowie die in Tabellen nochmals gesondert vorgestellten Zahlwörter werden dem hindisprachigen Benutzer eine wertvolle Hilfe beim Erlernen der deutschen Sprache sein.

Grammatischer Leitfaden des Hindi

Von Margot Gatzlaff-Hälsig.
5., durchgesehene und mit einer aktualisierten Einleitung versehene Auflage 2003. 197 Seiten.
978-3-87548-331-4. Kartoniert

Bereits seit mehr als 35 Jahren hat sich diese Grammatik für Hindilernende als zuverlässiges und unentbehrliches Hilfsmittel erwiesen.

Die wichtigsten grammatischen Regeln werden systematisch, ausführlich und wissenschaftlich fundiert dargestellt sowie anhand von vielen Beispielen aus der Umgangs- und Literatursprache veranschaulicht.

Deklinations- und Konjugationstabellen runden den Band ab.

Diese und viele andere Sprachlehrbücher und Nachschlagewerke erhalten Sie in jeder guten Buchhandlung und auf

BUSKE

buske.de